DRAMA IN THE CLASSROOM

Adapting and Preserving African Folktales into Plays by Teachers and Learners

TAKU VICTOR JONG

ISBN 979-8-89363-402-0

Dedication

I dedicate this book to my father, Mr Taku Peter Nembo, a seasoned teacher and educationist who initiated me to the art of storytelling, drawing and painting at a tender age. I also dedicate this book to my wife and children, who provided me with the moral and psychological support necessary during the period of research and writing. I cannot leave out primary and secondary teachers interested in exploiting their folklore and traditions as useful materials in the teaching and learning process.

Contents

▶ Contents ◀

▶ Contents ◀

Preface

The past four decades have witnessed decreasing interest in folktales and the storytelling event in many African countries. With the growing dominance of the television and internet, all eyes are now turned towards the television screen and the cell phone. There is also a growing social rift between parents and children because the evenings are no longer consecrated to narrating folktales which played a great role in the moral, social, academic and spiritual upbringing of children and youths in many African communities. The death of storytellers and griots that were admired for their talents and skills in narrating folk tales and other aspects of African culture has left a void in the process of production and transmission. Many school establishments and teachers who employed storytelling as a teaching technique and method of communication have abandoned the practice in favour of current prescribed pedagogic methods which provide no room for storytelling.

The main purpose of this study is not only to revive the storytelling event and interest in African folktales in the classroom; it is to reawaken the lost interest of teachers and parents and to remind them of the importance of stories and storytelling to the education and growth of the African child and youths not leaving out the cultivation of the collective memory of members in their respective communities.

In Part One, I have endeavoured to present the current state of oral narratives, adaptation and theatre in Cameroon. I have highlighted the damage caused by neglecting the storytelling event in homes and schools. I have also highlighted the importance of storytelling and what obtains in formal and informal settings. I have also presented the storytelling event vi-a-vis the theatre landscape, which is also witnessing a decline due to inadequate attention accorded by theatre lovers, teachers and theatre practitioners in Cameroon. The absence of storytelling and theatre at the basic and secondary levels of the Cameroon educational system is also identified as one of the major causes of the decline of the storytelling event and dwindling interest in folktales and other aspects of oral traditions of Cameroon and Africa in general. I have provided the views of some educationists, traditional leaders, and scholars who motivated and supported this project. I have provided practical ventures already carried out in adapting the Cameroonian oral tale for stage and screen in order to demonstrate what has been done by other scholars and adapting artists.

Part Two of the book presents a definition and broad perspective of the oral tale and the storytelling event. The definitions and views of scholars such as Isidore Okpewho(1990), Ibrahim Kashim Tala(2013), and Donna Rosenberg(1997) provide an understanding, role and functioning of the oral tale in Africa. Major aspects of the storytelling event such as the oral tale narrator and the audience have been present to reveal their importance in the storytelling and adaptation process.

In Part Three, the geographical, political and economic background and the chosen research methodology and theoretical standpoints have been pointed out to clarify where and how data was collected and analysed with the aid of field methodology such as observation, interview and administration of questionnaires. With the aid of research methods proposed by Kenneth Goldstein (1964), the formal, the highly-formal, the semi-formal and informal contexts, the artificial, and the induced natural contexts are analysed in detail to demonstrate how I went about collecting data in some villages and towns in the forests and grass fields of the South West and North West regions of Cameroon in Africa.

In the Part Four of the book, I have provided some major factors and justifications in favour of adapting the Cameroonian oral tale to play. These include a close regard of storytelling as a moralizing factor; storytelling as an educational and pedagogic tool; storytelling as a cultural and identity marker; the oral tale as cultural database; the oral tale and storytelling event as promoters of peace, unity, cooperation and solidarity; not leaving out the economic and therapeutic factors in favour of adapting and redynamising the Cameroonian tale in general.

Part Five is a practical demonstration of adapting the oral tale in a formal learning environment. In this section, I have demonstrated the role of the classroom teacher playing the role of the facilitator, the learners and adapting artist in adapting the selected tale: *Yomandene and the Stubborn Son* to play with the aid of Process Drama and the effective use of pedagogic applications. The proposals by

Paul Crimmens (2006) on the choice of class and students were useful in my choice of school and level of students for practical purposes. Proposals by Mike Peterson and Jennifer Hind (2005) on the teaching of folk tales such as information and lesson plans, specific activities and instructional strategies to teach; in addition to character development, setting, plot and themes were also exploited. I also explored the use of the K.W.L chart which explains the K-"What you know", the W-"What you want to learn" and the L-"What you have learned" to assist learners master the plot line. The effective use of Index Cards also assisted in the development of the plot. The Character Profile Chart led to the Character Development BioPoem and the title. The Bookman Strategy assisted learners remember the plot of the tale while the Inverted Pyramid explains the What, Who, Where, Why, When, and How of the plot. For the sake of community awareness and communication application, I have proposed a practical example of adapting the selected tale to radio and stage play.

The goal of this book is therefore to present the oral tale as an important aspect of the moral, socio-cultural, pedagogic, spiritual and economic development of children, the youths and adults of Cameroon and Africa in general. Secondly, the book has provided relevant justifications why the oral tale should be adapted to play. Lastly the book will serve as a practical guide to teachers at the basic, secondary and tertiary levels on how to adapt folk tales not only to plays in the classroom but in other forms such as film scripts, comic strips and documentaries.

Foreword

Drama in the Classroom: Adapting and Preserving African Folktales into Plays by Teachers and Learners is an important guide to teachers at all levels who have been battling with the task of exploiting local content in the teaching and learning process. The author has provided a practical approach to collecting folktales and adapting them to plays with the active participation of the learners. This book falls within the process of curriculum design, curriculum development and curriculum implementation within the context of rapid technological advancements in information and communication technologies. In an attempt to revive the storytelling event and render it as a useful method of teaching, the author has brought out the views of scholars, educationists and traditional leaders who support the fact that storytelling should be revived both in informal and formal learning environments. This book will be useful to teachers in teacher-training institutions, secondary schools and universities who are being drilled on the New Pedagogic Approach which encourages a learner-centred pedagogy that entails developing an inferential or critical thinking mind in the learner with competency generated through real life situations. With the aid of the teacher, the learners are not only encouraged to narrate folktales from their cultural settings, but also to transform these tales to plays with the aid of Process Drama which places the teacher more as a facilitator and guide during the adaptation process. Process Drama also encourages a systematic approach which respects Hilda Taba's (1962) curriculum design which begins with a careful diagnosis of needs, through a formulation of objectives, selection of content, organization of content, organization of learning activities and determining what to evaluate and the ways and means of doing it.

In an era where efforts towards the preservation of African oral narrative as an important aspect of African intangible cultural heritage via education are being promoted by UNESCO and other Non-governmental organisations, the need for trained and qualified teachers in the art of drama and adaptation will re-ignite the debate of reintroducing storytelling as an important pedagogic approach geared towards preserving the oral tale from annihilation.

The author has adopted a practical approach which if carefully followed by the teacher will go a long way to improve on the cognitive and creative skills of learners while making them useful participants in an adaptation process that preserves the Cameroonian oral tale in plays and the audio-visual media.

By Epah Fonkeng, Ph.D (Emeritus Professor of Education, University of Buea-Cameroon)

Acknowledgements

I hereby extend my sincere gratitude and appreciation to Emeritus Professor Nol Alembong, Emeritus Professor Charles Binam Bikoi, Emeritus Professor Tala Kashim Ibrahim and Emeritus Professor Epah Fonkeng for their immense contribution towards this project and my entire academic and professional journey. Their insightful comments and suggestions oriented and shaped some of the misconceptions that I encountered. My gratitude also goes to Professor, Dr. Zhao Baisheng of the Institute of World Literature at Peking University for his academic and moral support; to Professor Claudius Lazzeroni of Folkwang University and Thilo Grimm of the University of the Arts in Essen, Germany, for inviting me to carry out research in the Department of Design and the Essen-Duisburg Library in Germany. I cannot minimize the financial, material and moral support of Professor Scott Slovic, Editor of the Journal of Interdisciplinary Studies in Literature and Environment (ISLE) and to Professor Alfred Hornung, of English and Linguistics in Johannes Gutenberg University in Mainz, Germany. I also appreciate the contribution of staff and students of the Department of Performing and Visual Arts at the Faculty of Arts of the University of Buea, the University of Bloomsburg students and Form Three students of Government Secondary School Bwiyuku-Buea, for their active participation during the workshops lessons. I cannot forget the financial assistance given to me by the Ministry of Higher Education under the Research Mobility

Scheme to assist me carry out research in Germany. The moral and financial support of my parents, Mr. Taku Peter Nembo and Mrs. Chistiana Fiemna Taku; and Mr. Nkweta Jeremiah cannot be simplified.

The Current State of Oral Narratives, Adaptation and Theatre in Cameroon

Oral narratives have occupied and continue to occupy a primordial place in the literary culture and tradition of Africa. The oral tale is educative in nature, provides entertainment, and guarantees solidarity between the narrator and the audience. The tale has also been a vehicle of unity, peace and security and the transmission of valuable cultural heritage from one generation to the next. A major problem has been to guarantee the survival of these narratives in their original states and to assure their importance and value in the present context of globalisation, where different cultures are finding a place not only to exhibit their strength but to dominate weaker cultures. It is against this backdrop that this project is focused on adapting the oral tale to plays with the aid of Process Drama which involves the active participation of the teacher and learner in a formal learning environment. Recent developments in science and technology have led to a revolution in the fields of art, music, literature, traditional cultures and the worldview in many regions of Africa and other parts of the world. The proliferation of the written text, the influx of western and new forms of communication like the radio, television, internet, film and cinema alongside mobile telecommunication systems, assisted by satellite communication installations, have facilitated the movement of ideas, cultures and traditions from one part of the world to another. They have also diverted the attention of people, especially the youth in villages, towns and cities, from all that was formerly considered traditionally African. As a result, the oral tale, our prime focus, has lost its popularity and primordial place. The tale's social, economic, political and moral values are no longer held in high esteem in rural, semi-urban and urban areas.

The Current State of Oral Narratives

In Cameroon, where this study focuses, there is less emphasis on the oral tale and the storytelling event. The introduction of television signals and the creation of Cameroon Television Corporation (CTV) in 1985 attracted most families to the screen. Western and other foreign forms of lifestyle and entertainment in the form of theatre, music, film and dressing have found passage through the television. Gradually, television signals are getting to rural areas and villages, causing a shift similar to the one in towns and cities. Presently, the television, radio and the internet are the most popular media of information, entertainment and education in most African cosmopolitan contexts. As the demand for better standards of living, quest for education, jobs, leisure and comfort increases, the rate of rural exodus has also shot up. After a busy day's work on the part of parents and a tight learning schedule on the part of their children, the remaining evening hours are spent in front of the television or in some other form of relaxation. Consequently, there is little or no interpersonal communication between parents and children apart from the former giving instructions, orders and commands. The storytelling event which used to be an important aspect of entertainment, learning and morality, has now taken second stage in African traditional discourses. It is in this same vein that Nol Alembong (2011, p.15) identifies four story telling traditions in Africa: the dramatic presentations of stories, the tradition involving itinerant story tellers, the bardic tradition and the hearthside tradition. Alembong, while intimating that these traditions vary all over Africa, also states that they have many things in common especially as they relate to the objectives of performances. He cites Agatucci (2010) who states that in order to fully understand and appreciate African story telling traditions, there is need to study them in the context of the cultures which produce the stories. It is in the light of this assertion that the tales under adaptation have been chosen. They are destined for adaptation into plays, films and cartoons that capture the grass field and forest cultures of Cameroon within the ambit of globalisation. The tales which are founded on the aforementioned traditions have the capacity, if well dramatized and illustrated, to fit into the present audio-visual and communication technologies relevant for transmitting the tales, their messages and values to other parts of the globe without the displacement of the freelance artist, the itinerant story tellers, the bardos, or the narrator. Storytelling provides an opportunity for parents to come together not only to narrate stories but also to address issues affecting them as a community. The dances, songs and proverbs do not only build their minds; they also build their bodies. It is in this light that Robert J. Landy (1982) affirmed that tribal people all over the world employed dramatic dance to promote the mental health of members of their community. He cites the example of ancient Athenians who used it for both education and therapy. Rhetoric, a major component of storytelling, he intimates, was at the heart of medieval learning. Landy also points out that during the Renaissance the speaking of Latin and the stagings of plays were components of the school curriculum. As an example, he cites Mme de Maintenon, wife of Louis XIV, who established the Convent of Saint-Cy, where girls improvised dialogue and conversation; and also performed plays by Racine and Corneille. He laments that by the Nineteenth Century, however, drama in schools had dwindled to the production of the occasional school play.

In Cameroon the situation is not different. Dramatising the tale, for example, may not attract the attention it deserves because the literature curriculum in primary and secondary schools does not make provision for storytelling and theatre art as components of literary studies. The prescribed texts include plays written by Western playwrights such as William Shakespeare, Christopher Marlowe, Arthur Miller, William Congreve and Cameroonian playwrights such as Bole Butake, Sankie Maimo, Victor Elame Musinga, John Nkemngong Nkengasong, Anne Tanyi-Tang and others. Current Studies of selected plays focus on such aspects as plot, setting, characterization, dramatic dialogue, diction, dramatic action and meaning. Nothing is done to ensure that the plays are dramatized as part of the teaching requirement. In essence, theatre is completely absent. So, students go through the programme without mastering any skills in acting, memorization and dialogue.

The scenario is not different in Cameroonian universities where drama is also a component of literary studies. Here too, emphasis is placed on analysis and interpretation of play texts, poems and novels. Apart from the University of Yaoundé I where there exists a Unit of Performing Arts and Cinematography, the University of Buea which runs a Department of Performing and Visual Arts, alongside the universities of Dschang, and Douala, theatre as a subject is yet to be fully implanted in the academic programme in Cameroonian schools, colleges and universities. At the same time, the theatre-going public is non-existent. Apart from amphitheatres used as classrooms in state and private universities, and a few halls such as the Congress Halls in Yaoundé and Bamenda, the theatre space at the Goethe Institute and Former French Cultural Centre in Buea, there is no theatre hall built in respect of professional and international standards.

The relevance of storytelling and research on Cameroonian oral narratives has been dwindling progressively. Transmission and preservation are given little or no attention and the proliferation of Western and foreign cultural, linguistic and democratic principles have found safe grounds in Cameroon and other countries in Africa. The storytelling event which played an important role in the social integration and unity of Africans has been abandoned for newer Western and other foreign forms of entertainment and communication. Preliminary questions posed to some Cameroonian youths born after 1980 and the answers provided revealed that most of them cannot recount any story learned either at school or during evening gatherings with family, friends and relatives. Their knowledge is related to stories from textbooks in the curriculum and other societal happenings. Questions posed to adults above forty revealed that people within this age bracket have forgotten the majority of tales narrated to them while growing up in the villages and semi-urban settings. They regret that the storytelling event in the past that involved a performer or a storyteller and an audience with all the traditional paraphernalia involved no longer attract their attention. Many students in Cameroonian primary and secondary schools also confessed that stories in the written text are no longer interesting because they are void of pictures and illustrations.

Ruth Finnegan (1970) points out that the oral literacy tradition of Africa was dying out with the impact of literate, wealthier and more progressive cultures. Finnegan also affirmed that importance was placed on political songs, new versions of dance, songs and lyrics, the written word and auditory forms. She expressed worry that the written word may not play an important role in the development of Africa in the future. In order to remedy this situation, she appealed for further research in these subjects and finally proposes drama as one of the special forms of the storytelling event. It is this call which we have heeded, in order to propose ways of giving new vigour to this culture and literary tradition once held in high esteem. She finally calls on critics and observers of African film to heed the lesson rather than "limping off" to Hollywood or to Europe to seek models. The urgency to revive the storytelling event and spark the interest in oral tales is supported by Bruce

A. Rosenberg (1987) while reaffirming the importance of a face-to-face situation provided by the storytelling event affirms that:

> While literature has made many aspects of culture available to a very great proportion of society's members, the impersonality of print has also made culture easy to avoid. Print removes a portion of learning from that immediate chain of personal confrontations.---Plato had argued that the wisdom of writing was superficial; no give and take of cross-examination and responses was possible. If the reader questions a written proposition, there can be no response, no defense. A book can be put aside; it may never be opened at all. Discussion, argument, and oral deliberation are not easily side-stepped in face-to-face situations. (p.76)

Kashim Ibrahim Tala (1999) also laments that oral narratives are still at the stage at which Europeans left them centuries ago. Tala states that the images and symbols used by narrators were conceived a long time ago and affirms that today creativity cannot be associated with traditional artists. What exist, according to him, are improvisations, adjustments, trimmings and impositions. He also laments that the death and disappearance of honest storytellers, the present corrupt and negative influence of money, tribalism and a rising decline of creativity and ingenuity which do not inspire modern researchers to record tales in traditional settings. He points out that those who have embarked on this research have discovered that a particular version of a tale may just be a reflection of the kinds of tips and motivation given to the storyteller and the audience in that particular community.

At a pedagogic level, some observations are worth mentioning. As a Form Two Literature teacher-in-practice at the Government Bilingual High School in Yaoundé-Cameroon, I observed that whenever I assigned students to read and respond to questions related to Ngoh Agnes Nzuh's *Tales from the Forest and Grass fields*, some of them were either distracted or bored, while others gave up the exercise and dozed off. On the other hand, when I asked those who had lost interest in the exercise to dramatise some of the movements, words and actions of birds and animals in animal stories, for instance, the learners became more active.

Noupea Nkayimbo Margaret Assumpta, a Form Three teacher of English Language and Literature at Government Secondary School Bwiyuku in the South West Region of Cameroon revealed in a chat with this researcher some of her experiences in teaching tales found in some prescribed textbooks and readers of the curriculum. She observed that the students are bored reading long stories void of pictures, drawings or illustrations. She also pointed out that they also found it difficult to recount parts of the tale vividly because of a lack of side attractions. On a happy note, she revealed that whenever she attempted to mimic the movements, actions and words of some of the characters in animal stories, the students became alert and attentive. The class also became livelier when two or more students were called to dramatise the roles of these animal characters in front of the class. The evaluation at the end of the lesson revealed startling results in terms of content and subject mastery. She finally applauded the efforts of Nzuh in providing drawings of scenes, actions and characters at various stages in each of her tales. She concluded by praising her efforts at writing tales of readable lengths, which helped in holding and keeping the attention of the students.

It is therefore not surprising when Balbina Ebong laments that a look through the contents of *Go for English* at the level of "Terminale" reveals the complete absence of folktales, either from the Cameroonian society or elsewhere, in spite of the abundance of folktales in Cameroon and their significance in language teaching and learning. Such a worry is shared by this researcher who taught *Go For English* to second-language learners of English in Francophone Secondary Schools. I share Ebong's worry that many textbooks that are used for language teaching and learning in Cameroonian schools hardly reflect the learner's environment in terms of culture and literature. This goes against the prescription of the current syllabus that recommends the use of local cultural material by teachers in English language and literature. It has been observed that many teachers do not use stories because they consider storytelling a time- consuming task that slows and affects their coverage of the school curriculum. At this juncture, I discovered with dismay the little attention given to the study of children literature in Cameroon schools and colleges, a negligent and slow integration of indigenous knowledge in Cameroon's formal education curriculum, the absence of practical research in oral literature by scholars and students in Cameroonian universities and the absence of a culture that valorises the oral tale and heritage of Cameroon.

At the local level, the storytelling event has been replaced by the radio, television, internet and cell-phone culture. At the end of a busy day in the farms and offices, most parents find it difficult to assemble their children after an evening meal to tell stories. It is important to note that these recent forms, apart from informing its audience on current happenings and events, have brought the world of music, cinema and sports closer to the audience. Unfortunately, their attractive nature has distanced the youths from their parents, culture and role models. In an interview with Fon Angwafor III in the Mankon palace in Bamenda, he lamented that whenever he called upon his children to narrate stories and teach them important aspects of the tradition and culture, they were either found glued to the television screen or engaged in some other form of entertainment generally connected to the Western culture. He also affirmed they were more interested in the white man's culture transmitted mostly by the lone television screen in his palace. He lamented that he felt so estranged, especially from the young generation who copy models from the West.

On the death of the storytelling event and the damage that this has caused on his community, Fon Angwafor lamented that the society was changing to the detriment of his country, Cameroon. He said that the citizens speak English and French and not their local languages. According to him, language was an element of a culture. So, by adopting English and French, Cameroonians have become foreigners in their homeland. He intimated that the customs and traditions of the colonial masters seem to be gaining more grounds than the authentic culture and traditions of Cameroonians. He also decried the fact that the system of education being practiced in Cameroon was and remains foreign. He said that storytelling was an important aspect of education and intimated that in the distant past, children were educated by teachers through storytelling with the teachers posing as parents. He recalled that when the children listened to these tales, they were anxious and inquisitive. Today, he laments that there has been a dramatic change. He pointed out that all the attention of his children and even parents is on the television, which according to him is also foreign. He decried the fact that those who operate these television stations are guided by foreign ideas and have been taught and trained to execute and appreciate what the makers of the television want.

Fon Angwafor also regretted that the television and radio are used to denigrate the culture of Cameroon. He referred to the exercise of crowning or honouring those who have achieved something great with a bird's feather as a mark of recognition but which is considered today as primitive. In the past, he said it was a source of inspiration to hunters and warriors to lure them towards success. He lamented that journalists over the radio and television even question the raison d'être of the red feather as an instrument of recognition. He also pointed out that every aspect of Cameroon's culture is being mocked by his children. He goes further to decry the fact that many talented citizens have been educated to transmit what they learned in western oriented institutions. He also lamented that many have not been educated to carry out research in their home country in order to effectively contribute to nation building.

Fon Angwafor further blamed the kinds of textbooks being used in our schools. According to him, they are tailored to meet the needs of American and European thoughts. He wondered where the original thoughts of Africans are in the minds of the teachers in Cameroonian schools. He also lamented that everything was now formal. He also observed that the university degree and not morality is respected. He castigated the fact that teachers have been brought up to despise African culture and tradition. According to him, if storytelling worked, it is because it had no rival. Unfortunately, much research has not been carried out on it. He also bemoaned the fact that storytelling was not on the syllabus and curriculum and did not even seem to be of interest to writers and researchers. He feared that before long, Cameroonians will be considered neither Africans, Europeans nor Americans. On a final note, he recommended that if there were any ways in which the Cameroonian culture could find expression through the television, he would not spare any effort to support such an endeavour.

In an interview with Mr. Gobu Daniel, former Head Teacher of Presbyterian School Mbesoh–Bamessing-Ndop in the North West Region of Cameroon, the teacher and school administrator observed that some teachers dwell much time on storytelling while others allowed the pupils to speak the vernacular in class. According to him, this has a little disadvantage because children came to school to learn English and not the vernacular. He also observed that many parents did not see the importance of storytelling in school since they consider it to have a place in the home. He also said that as a teacher and father, he told a few stories to his children. But with the coming of the television and internet, he lamented that many around him now spend their evenings watching movies on television.

In an interview with Wendy Litumbe Ebenezer, a notable of the Bakweris of Buea, he recalled that his parents had embraced Christianity and the white man's language as far back as 1925 when he was born. So, storytelling according to him is lost because children today do not know their language prior to school-going age. He affirmed that as an individual, all his children went to school without learning their language. In this wise he pointed out that it was difficult to sit with elders and listen to these stories which were mostly narrated in their local languages. When asked if storytelling was part of the school curriculum when he went to school, he intimated that they had stories in the school different from what were narrated at home. He regretted that since 1955 when his first son was born, he never sat him down to tell stories. On a sad note, he affirmed that storytelling had died in his house a long time ago. He also attributed the death of storytelling to the coming of radio and television. He said they were not good pedagogic tools used to pass on the stories to the younger generation. According to him, most of them who have never been to school will not be able to listen to or watch and interpret the stories being aired. Those who are illiterates only watch the pictures on the screen without understanding what they are conveying. So the new media, according to him, only serve the learned, especially in urban settings.

The work invites the innovative use of technology in the transmission process. This comes with some advantages and disadvantages. The play script derived from the process of adaptation will ultimately invite the skills and expertise of a play director, actors and a technical crew responsible in putting the play on stage. With the aid of relevant sound, light, costumes and props, new challenges of adaptation for stage will be posed. A similar process will be required at the level of producing the adapted script to a movie. The demands of the film production crew expose some of the challenges of adapting for film. It is worth noting that the use of technology, while rendering the tale available in different audio-visual media, will render the tales more useful and relevant.

Snippets of Adaptation

The process of adaptation for stage and screen is evident in *Zintgraff and the Battle of Mankon* by Bole Butake and Gilbert Doho. The play is an epic adaptation of the history of Cameroon during the German colonial epoch from 1884 to 1919. It was adapted for stage by Bole Butake and Gilbert Doho, playwrights and theatre activists. The story depicts the role played by Doctor Eugene Zintgraff during the German colonial era in Cameroon. The play is a historical presentation of a series of wars fought between the Bafut people led by their Fon, Abumbi I, and the Germans backed by neighbouring tribes like Bali and Mankon. The play points to the relationship between Zintgraff and the Fon of Bafut during these troubled years. It is important to note that history holds that the Germans found it difficult to defeat the Bafut people. A case in point is in 1891, wherein the German forces from Bali Nyonga attacked Mankon in revenge to the death of two messengers sent to Bafut to demand Ivory. This led to the burning down of the town of Mankon by the Germans on January 31, 1891. In retaliation, warriors from Bafut and Mankon attacked the Germans and inflicted heavy losses on them in what has been referred to as "The Battle of Mankon". Paul Nkwi (1989) reports that the Bafut people launched a bloody battle against the Germans that saw the withdrawal of Bali and the two German expeditions led by Dr. Zintgraff and his 170 natives.

In 2012, two Cameroonians, Godwin Nganah and Musing Derick, movie producer and director respectively, succeeded to adapt the historical account into a film shot in Ngoketunjia Division of the North West Region of Cameroon as a TV series involving over 200 persons as actors, crew members, technicians and supporting artists. The process of moving from stage to film is tasking and costly but brings the incidents as closer to reality as possible. With the aid of cinematographic and camera techniques, for example, the scenes of killings, hangings and murders are clearly brought out in film than on stage. The bloody encounters between the German forces and the Bafut warriors are easily captured in film than stage. During an interview with Musing Derick, he said that they had to pay a series of visits to Bafut and Bali, especially to the palaces to get relevant information on the dressing and speech patterns of the people during the period of German annexation. In one of his visits, he learnt that the warriors wore *sanjas,* specifically to cover their nakedness and spoke in their vernacular. He also said that while in Bali, he also learnt that the fon of Bali, for example, had supernatural powers and could easily transform himself into a lion when he got angry. Such a claim was believed although none was alive to attest to it. Derrick also said that in Bafut, the fon was not only the military leader but was considered as a spiritual commander. It was believed that the fon could appear in different places at the same time. He also learnt that as far as the war was concerned, there was no direct physical confrontation between the German soldiers and the Bafut warriors. He pointed out that there were a series of ambushes and kidnappings characterized by hits-and-runs. On this note, he advised young writers, film makers and historians to revisit oral and historical sources, and custodians of the culture to obtain vital information that could enrich their stories. On the process of adaptation, he intimates that the adapter must be faithful to the original source text when fictionalizing it. In essence, he proposes a ten percent adaptation and ninety percent originality and advises that we remain faithful to the source text so that we are not accused of distorting the facts. It is in this wise that adaptation could serve not only as a medium of preservation but as a facilitator of communication and transmission.

The process of adaptation is clearly explained by Naomi Epongse Nkealah (2011) when she states that Butake uses historical material as building blocks to construct new understandings of contemporary society. On this notes, she affirms that:

> *For the dramatist, as Michael Etherton (1982:144) notes, history provides not only stories and themes which are specific to the dramatist's world view but also specific content, in terms of the playwright's own society, which embodies these broad themes. --- However, one has to exercise caution here lest one be tempted to view historical draw as a reflection of "true" historical experiences. --- Historical drama can, therefore, only lay claim to possible interpretations of the past, but in using history as its major component it emphasizes the importance of memory as a national archive. (195)*

Adapting the play, based on historical events that characterized the German colonial experience, provided an opportunity by both playwrights not only to revisit history but to educate the audience about events they did not have the opportunity to live. This reveals the power of drama in the process of recreating true historical events.

Another historical play adapted for stage is Victor Epie Ngome's *What God has put Asunder.* It is an adaptation of the post-independence period of British Southern Cameroon in 1961 and the referendum of 1972 that led to the birth of a unitary state of Cameroon. The play reveals the co-existence of British Southern Cameroons and the Republic of Cameroon leading to the period of the Founbam Conference when both parties decided to live as one entity in what is now term the Re-unification of Cameroon or the peaceful revolution. In an attempt at adapting the play for stage, Ngome invokes the marriage metaphor of two incompatible entities. Ngome in this metaphor presents

Weka as former Southern Cameroons, Miche Garba as "La Republique du Cameroun", the British government as Weka's parents, and Reverend Gordon and the Orphanage standing for U.N. Trusteeship Mandate over Southern Cameroons. On the other hand, Louis represents France, and Emeka stands for Nigeria, who also posed as another suitor. Weka prefers Garba but soon discovers that Garba is only interested in exploiting the cocoa farms left behind by Weka's father. With the aid of dialogue and characters whose names are symbolic references of the countries where they hail from, Ngome re-enacts the relationship that existed between "La Republic du Cameroun" and West Cameroon after Independence through to Re-unification. For example, the name Emeka is a typical Ibo name common amongst Eastern Nigerians who carried out trade in the English speaking regions of Cameroon. Mention of the name Emeka, immediately tells any member of audience living in the English speaking part of Cameroon that he hails from Nigeria. Any Cameroonian who hears the name 'Garba' immediately realizes that it is a name common amongst the Hausas and Fulanis of the Northern Regions of Cameroon. Louis is a popular French name while Gordon is a typical English name. So from the aforementioned names, we can immediately link the character to the country where he or she hails from. This is a technique used by most adapting playwrights. The plantation metaphor of the cocoa farms represents the rich cocoa, rubber, palms, tea and banana plantations that were opened by the British before the independence of Cameroon. The mention of the collapse of the cooperative society brings back memories of the reckless mismanagement of the former National Produce

Marketing Board by managers from "La Republique du Cameroun". This study deviates from the use of metaphor in exposing socio-political realities to the production of intangible cultural data that can serve educational, moral and environmental purposes.

Another example that came to light is the television documentary on the Bakweri armed resistance directed by George Ngwane and Kome Epie Mathias. This is an adaptation of the legend, Kuva Likenye, a Bakweri hero who resisted the Germans from having complete control of the land of Buea. In a series of mock actions by actors, interviews, drawings and sketches, Ngwane and Kome successfully revisit the conflicts that marked the German conquest of Buea. With the aid of a narrator, the story is recounted accompanied by pictures, drawings and illustrations. The approach is more interactive and brings to the viewer's testimonies of life accounts of the events as narrated to the writer by custodians of the tradition. With the aid of songs, animated drawings and simulation, the producer was able to re-enact the life and heroic deeds of Kuva Likenye. Mola Njoh Litumbe, one of the interviewees, recounted the origin of the crisis, which was basically around land ownership. According to Njoh Litumbe the Bakweris fought to be recognized as owners of the land and those exploiting the land to pay royalties. In thirty minutes, the documentary recounts the events leading up to the conflict and the personal exploits of Kuva Likenye who was assisted by a group of untrained warriors armed with bows and arrows to resist the German exploitation of the Bakweri people and land in what has been considered the Bakweri-German Wars of 1891 to 1894.

Taiwo Oloyede (1967) cites Amos Tutuola, Chinua Achebe, Cyprian Ekwensi, Camara Laye, Mongo Beti, J.P. Clark and Wole Soyinka as those who draw freely from oral traditions and thus their works are culturally relevant to everyday life. Taiwo intimates that this influence is not likely to predominate in the future. It is hoped that it will always have some impact on West African writing, thus preserving contact with the cultural roots of the people. According to Taiwo, Tutuola has shown how old tales can be translated to a new context. Achebe according to him has given some indications how proverbs, tales, myths can be successfully exploited to give authenticity and beauty to the West African novel. Soyinka, he intimates, has shown that old beliefs can be the subject of brilliant drama while Clark in his verse has demonstrated how the African traditional way of life forms a perfect setting for heroic poetry. Taiwo affirms that these writers have shown the potentialities of African folklore and mythology as a vitalizing force in West African literature.

Ukachi Nnenna and Chisimdi Udoka (2010) answering the question: "why do creative artists find other people's works appealing, refer to Yerima who states that it is a matter of "choice", which is linked to the interest or "likeness" or even "fondness" for an older work based on the immediacy of the themes of an old work. They also point to the achievement of such a work, the urgency to update such a work and the relationship between the older artist and the adapting artist. Therefore, adapting for stage is based on the close relationship that play directors share with storytellers.

Things Fall Apart, according to Ukachi and Chisimdi, can he considered as a novel that continue to attract adapting artists. Firstly, they claim that it is based on a true story of the Igbo society in the early years of contact with the white man. According to them, the story could have remained in its original form and handed down by way of mouth from one generation to the next. But Chinua Achebe, who they consider as the first adapting artist, falling in love with the story, decided to preserve it in his novel, *Things Fall Apart*. They intimate that the Igbos are presented as a people with great institutions, traditions and laws that valorize justice, fairness and hard work, and with a firm belief in the supremacy of God. The novel which is an adaptation of a lone story that alludes to the path underwent by the Igbo society during the colonial epoch, in the words of Ukachi and Chisimdi *"is an attempt at repairing some of the damage done to Ndi Igbo in particular and Africans in general by European depictions "*(126). Other adapting artists inspired by Achebe's descriptions have taken the story to the film media inspired by Achebe's novel art. According to Ukachi and Chisimdi, the film version of *"Things Fall Apart"* came out in 1987, directed by David Orere, was shot on celluloid and transferred to tapes for the traditional small screen of the television for Nigerian viewers, featuring Pete Edochie as Okonkwo.

Ukachi and Chisimdi recommend that fidelity in adaptation is to the spirit and not the letter, nor to structure or to dialogue. They quote Achebe in an interview with Jerome Brooks of the Paris Review (2011) saying:

I believe in the complexity of the human story and that there's no way you can tell the story in one way and say, this is it. Always there will be someone who can tell it differently depending on where they are standing; the same person telling the story will tell it differently. I think of that masquerade in Igbo festivals that dances in the public arena. The Igbo people say, if you want to see it well, you must not stand in one place. The masquerade is moving through this big arena, dancing!. If you are rooted to a spot, you miss a lot of the grace. So you keep moving, and this is the way I think the world's stories should be told from many different perspectives. (138)

In essence the novel has the capacity to lend itself into any medium and enable the spread of its message to a wider public. It is in this vein that George Nyamndi adapts *Things Fall Apart* into *Things Fall in Place*. He provides an answer to why he chose Achebe's novel as the basis of his adaptation when he responds categorically:

Firstly the novel spoke to me in a very immediate way as it ought to speak to every African. Andl thought that the best way of indicating my own appreciation to Achebe was in diversifying the pedagogic potentials of the novel. Because it is not only literature but also a therapeutic instrument for Africans; a narrative that speaks to our sense of pride. Now, if we leave it to the novel's sphere only, it will not reach out to as many readers as its importance warrants. And so I thought that if we could place it on stage, we would by so doing be diversifying its potential to reach out to a large public and to make its message a lot more immediate than it is in narrative form because you know that theatre is lot more direct and more powerful in its message delivery potential than the novel because in the former you come face-to-face with re-enacted reality or re-enacted problems and challenges. That way you can gauge the importance of that narrative immediately without flipping pages upon pages. (G. Nyamndi, personal communication, February 25,2015).

Nyamndi also states that the novel is addressed to Africans in general and the more people it reaches, the more its relevance. It is for this reason that he prefers theatre which according to him is more direct and powerful than film. He also affirms that theatre enables you to come face to face with re-enacted reality or re-enacted problems and challenges. When questioned if he brought new elements into the play during the adaptation process, Nyamndi states:

Yes, certainly. For things to fall in place, you have to make them fall in place.

And so in "Things Fall in Place", at the end of the play, a memorial is founded in honour of Okonkwo, The Okonkwo Memorial, which is a school where the likes of his son, Nwoye, who could not go to school because of his father's trenchant opposition to Western values, can now attend school. Do not forget that everybody in Things Fall Apart is a symbol and that little boy carries with him some of the tragedies that we see in African societies today, such as the denial of access to education for reasons which are usually untenable. Ikemefuna and other little children are sacrificed on the altar of practices in today's world that have little or no locus standi. In Things Fall in Place, we pull all the parts together in this memorial. So we can say that Okonkwo lived for an ideal, that ideal not being necessarily what he thought it to be but rather what the society that lived after him said it was. The Okonkwo Memorial is built with the money used to obtain temporary release of the village elders. That's the money which goes into that project. So in essence, what we are saying here is that Africans are really the authors of their own destinies. (G. Nyamndi, personal communication, February 25,2015).

Such is the poetic licence that adapting artists enjoy in the process of rendering the source text more relevant in the present dispensation.

It is important to note how this research endeavour departs from what has been previously carried out by other researchers and artists mentioned above. Firstly, this study opens a new page on the need to preserve Cameroonian intangible heritage, especially the oral tale, presently threatened by extinction because of the influence of western culture, especially stories that have been transformed into stage plays, movies and cartoons through colourful story books, movies and cartoons and transmitted via the radio, television and internet. Secondly the study demonstrates practically, with the aid of illustrations and pictures different parameters and techniques of transforming the Cameroonian oral tale to plays through a process of adaptation. The technique of adaptation has been used to change the form of the source tale to a more dynamic story characterised by setting, dramatic dialogue, characterisation, structure, and diction. Thirdly, the study points to the need of creating tangible cultural data in the form of plays that could also be produced and transported to the global cultural market through colourful story books, movies and cartoons with the aid of the television and internet not only to face the present wave of competition but to display the Cameroonian cultural product to other cultural adherents and different peoples of the world.

Faced with an influx of western movies and comics characterised by violence, intrigues and manipulation, the study further points at the relevance of the Cameroonian oral tale replete with moral lessons useful not only to children, but to the present generation of youths and adults saddled by western forms of entertainment, lifestyle and influence. It therefore opens a new window for the adaptation of tales that will serve as a counter dialogue to the devastating influence of some western and other foreign stories.

The study goes further to point out the fact that there are new settings, especially in towns and cities in Africa and Cameroon in particular which the oral tale can find expression and whose inhabitants are crippled by individualism and the quest for wealth leaving parents and elders with little or no time to assemble as a family to tell stories and also to hand down moral instructions. Dominated by the audiovisual media of instruction and entertainment, there is therefore need to adapt tales with moral and spiritual values that can be transmitted through the television and internet.

Lastly the study opens a new wave for the production of cultural content in the face of the digital switch over from analogue to digital which necessitates the availability of many television channels propelled by satellite and the optic fibre currently being installed in different parts of Cameroon. The adaptation of selected Cameroonian oral tales to plays, film scripts and comic strips will guarantee the availability of the relevant content highly needed by play, film and cartoon directors and artists for entertainment and commercial purposes destined for television houses and internet. Theatre is yet to gain solid grounds in Cameroon. With the existence of a few university theatre troupes whose activities are limited to staging plays in the university, schools and other public events organized by the Ministry of Culture, the Ministry of Environment, Nature Protection and Sustainable Development, the Ministry of Forestry and Wildlife, the Canadian High Commission and the American Cultural Centre, the impact of theatre is yet to be felt. The use of theatre as means of education, sensitization, conscientisation and promotion of values in the community is yet to be enforced. Apart from Hansel Ndumbe Eyoh's *Hammocks to Bridges (1986)* which involved the use of theatre as a tool for educating the forest populations of Kurume in the South West Region, the practical application of theatre for development in the Noni fondom and other parts of the North West Region supervised by Bole Butake, the use of theatre as a cultural, political, educational and moral tool is yet to the fully implemented in Cameroon. Eyoh intimates that theatre involves the viewer, encourages him to objectify his responses to given situations rather than talking down to viewers as in a talk-show, and provides a forum in which people talk to people and comment on everyday issues with the aid of a fictional situation that allows for the handling of even sensitive and controversial issues.

The proposal made by Eyoh on the possibility of creating dramas within urban and rural communities using real-life characters to dramatize their own lives on a wide range of subjects such as agriculture, community, planned parenthood, environmental protection and improvement, nutrition and home economics, women's education, arts and crafts, culture, management and leadership within story lines with strong dramatic force, has not been systematically implemented either at institutional, state or private levels. As the years go by, other issues such as the protection of the girl child, labour rights, cyber-crime, terrorism, homosexuality, lesbianism, corruption, unemployment, and AIDS have cropped up. Yet theatre, with all its potentials, has not been fully exploited to address the aforementioned issues in private and public spaces.

The Theatre Scenario in Cameroon

Hansel Ndumbe Eyoh, Bole Butake, Gilbert Doho, Asheri Kilo and Oyie-Ndzie Polycarpe, Cameroonian theatre teachers and practitioners paint a picture of theatre activities that animated and continue to animate the theatre landscape of Cameroon. They point to the Ensemble National, founded in 1977 as the country's largest and most active production company with separate groups working in dance, drama and music. They point out that this group thrilled their audience using their orchestra which includes different sizes and styles of drums, string instruments, bow-lutes, raffles, clappers, whistles, xylophones, horns and trumpets, accompanied by costumes for ensemble performances which include fine headgear, masks, huge dress patterns including material from tree bark, animal skins, cotton, raffia, leaves, feathers and cowries. They carried out public performances mainly in the French-speaking part of the country, especially in the French Cultural Centres in Yaoundé and Douala, the American Cultural Centre in Yaoundé and in various colleges and church halls around the country. It is important to note that close to 40 years on, this scenario has not changed. These centres and public spaces continue to host a series of planned and organized performances.

They also observed that another troupe that championed theatre performances not only in the university milieu, but also in schools and public spaces was the Yaoundé University Theatre. Eyoh, Kilo and Butake also state that Jacqueline Leloup of French origin was instrumental in the development of theatre in the University of Yaounde. According to them, she created the Club d'Art Dramatique

(Dramatic Arts Club) which was latertransformed into the Théâtre Universitaire (University Theatre). This was followed shortly by the creation of an English section by Hansel Ndumbe Eyoh, a playwright and theatre animator. They go further to point out that Leloup and Eyoh staged a number of plays and animated the theatre landscape, and intimated that after the return of Leloup to France and the appointment of Eyoh as Director of Cultural Affairs in the Ministry of Information and Culture, Gilbert Doho and Bole Butake replaced them. They go further to state that Butake maintained Eyoh's small production tradition while Doho turned his group into a more socially committed company. By 1990, for financial reasons, these groups could no longer fund their activities. They also pointed out that due to the growing argument for Anglophone Rights, the university's support for theatre was seen as anti-government. With the wind of change blowing across Africa and the rising call for multi-party democracy, any theatrical piece that went against government's interest was considered subversive.

Apart from the role of the Yaoundé University Theatre, they list a host of earlier theatre troupes in Yaoundé that contributed to the theatre movement by staging plays mostly at the French Cultural Centre. These include the Associations des Jeunes Artistes Cameroonais (Association of Young Cameroonian Artists), a troupe founded by playwright-director Stanislas Owona; Le Negro Star (Negro Star) founded by Adolphe Mballa; L'Avant–Garde Africaine (African Avant-Garde) founded by Dikongue Pipa; Les Compagnons de la Comédia (Comedy Companions) founded by Marcel Mvondo; and the most ambitious of the groups, Les Trétaux d'ébène (Ebony stage) by Charles Nyalle;

Les Etudiants Associés (Associated students) by playwright, Raymond Ekossono, les Etudiants du Renouveau (New Deal Students) by Rabiatou Njoya; Le Théâtre Saissonier (Seasonal Theatre) by Lucien Mamba; and the Flame Players founded in 1988 by Godfrey Tangwa. They also point to the fact that several actors in the Ensemble National also created occasional groups such as Keki Manyo's Les Perles Noires (Black Pearls) which staged mostly foreign plays from school syllabuses. Apart from this array of troupes, mostly in Yaoundé, they point to the Musinga Drama Group founded in 1974 by Victor Elame Musinga which animated and continue to promote theatre in the South West Region of Cameroon especially in schools and local communities.

It is important to note that most of these troupes staged either Western plays or plays and sketches written by the troupes' directors. Their audience was limited to those present in the theatre hall. With little collected as gate takings, and with little financial assistance either from the University or the Ministry of Culture, most of these groups dissipated as the actors sought for greener pastures either abroad or in the public service. Theatre therefore became a past-time or hobby to most of the actors, who squeezed time off their daily schedules to attend rehearsals. Active theatre activities and production could be seen in the theatre troupes lodged mainly in the universities and cultural centres. Transforming the tales into plays for primary and secondary schools and for community outreach may provide other means for the dissemination and transmission of Cameroon's cultural heritage and values.

PART TWO

Defining and Understanding the Oral Tale and the Storytelling Event

The Oral Tale

To understand the major issues being discussed in this work, it will be important to define and situate the term "oral tale", commonly referred to as oral narrative within the context of this study. Although many definitions have been advanced of the term, we will still propose others based on our study. Oral narratives can be myths, legends, proverbs and riddles. They are generally composed and transmitted by word of mouth. Kashim Ibrahim Tala (1999) defines the oral tale as a work of art, a mirror of life and an intellectual exercise. He provides its defining characteristics which make the oral tale fictional and secular, transmitted by the personal word of mouth, ephemeral and whose existence and continuity can be assured when realised in an oral communicative process. He sees performance, which involves face-to-face contact between a performer and an audience, as integral to the whole concept of the oral tale. This also ties with the elements of orature which, according to him, include oral composition, oral performance and oral transmission.

Tala intimates that:

> *Among a youthful audience however, the oral narrative is used to promote the positive values of the society. That is, the oral narrative is used as an instrument for indirectly socialising the youth to the dynamics of cultural practice. Thus; while the oral narrative serves to teach the young, it is utilised to refresh the minds of adults of the potentials within the framework of community-individual dialectic. (84)*

The above analysis brings us to the values which the present youthful generation in Cameroon and Africa stand to acquire if African prose narratives are brought back into the limelight.

The folktale, according to Tala (2013) is the most popular form of oral literature in Cameroon, the first thing to be discovered by students of oral literature and the only form on which so much has been written and published over the years. Tala states that where myths and legends are preoccupied with history or with the explanation of natural phenomena, folktales deal with the familiar and the fantastic. Tala also affirms that "folktales serve the villagers as means of entertainment, emotional release and avenues of acculturation of young people" (43). Under the folktale Tala identifies the animal tales, tricksters' tales, aetiological tales, monster tales and tales about people. These different types are not confined to specific frames. It is therefore common to find an aspect overlapping in a different type or version of the oral tale.

Islidore Okpewho (1990) considers *oral literature* as the most commonly used term for the subject and defines it as "literature delivered by word of mouth"(3). *Orature*, he goes further to say, is a current but seldom used term that emphasizes the oral character of the literature. Okpewho considers 'the folk' as the creators of this literature, commonly considered as uneducated people who dwell in villages or rural communities. But such an assumption has now been challenged; for, as Okpewho states that:

> *Nowadays we collect some of our most exciting pieces of oral literature from performers who live in cities and some not-so-rustic towns who have at least a primary school education and have travelled far and wide (even outside Africa) with their performances.(4)*

This is apt because a host of my informants are literate, including retired civil servants, teachers, educated traditional rulers and retired politicians. David Buchan considers folk literature as folk culture and a 'register of culture' maintained and transmitted primarily by word of mouth and customary practice. He describes it in other terms as the 'literature of folk culture' transmitted by verbal means rather that by manuscript or print. At this stage, the material is preserved by a series of verbal processes which involve the narrator(s) and the audience. Buchan intimates that its verbal nature is not to say that it never reaches manuscript or print. According to him, oral literature naturally finds itself in print but its status as folk literature does not diminish, and it does not suddenly metamorphose into high literature since the material still continues to be transmitted by the traditional verbal and aural medium. It is on this note that Joe Winston considers folktales to be ancient and contain similar patterns of fantasy, symbol and magic, forming part of an oral, folk tradition but with central protagonists who originate from humble backgrounds. This definition is apt but controversial in the sense that the existence of the folk is not an issue of the past. The folk is any grouping of human beings with shared interests and values. The folk are found in both rural and urban areas playing different roles. Their actions and activities are subject to examination and analysis. Their lives constitute a series of tales either told by them or about them. To relegate the notion of folk to ancient settings is to deny the existence of different communities involved in different activities in diverse social settings. Today the folk is no longer the illiterate farmer or servant in a distant community but a cream of retired engineers, civil servants or teachers who once played significant and important roles in their respective places of work. As part of the folk, and with so much experience and knowledge, their stories are bound to enrich the intangible cultural heritage in their respective societies.

Rosenberg (1997) defines a folktale as a story which in its plot is pure fiction that has no particular location in either time or place. He adds that despite its elements of fantasy, a folktale is actually a symbolic way of presenting the various means by which human beings cope with the world in which they live. He goes further to state that they concern people or animals that speak and act like people. He also points to the fact that folktales are entertaining and have a universal and lasting appeal, relate to human beings across time and space, provide man with the encouragement and tools to forge his path, have moral themes and in Western cultures have contributed to a national sense of identity and pride. These stories, according to him, compel us to consider who we are, where we come from and where we are going. They also instil a spirit of respect, cooperation and understanding between the younger and older generations, between parents and their children and finally between citizens and state institutions.

Silvano Galli(1983) in his research on the folktale in Anyi-Bona Society states that:

> The collection and interpretation of the traditional folktales allows us not only to know the traditional society, but even to prose, starting on solid foundations, some ways to build a modern culture through the influence of the tale on the theatre, movies, television, novels and songs. (13)

The importance of African tales and other prose narratives, their relevance in seeking common grounds between traditions and cultures of diverse ethnic, national and internal values lead us to an examination of the tale under study with a view to proposing ways and means of transforming them to play so that the tale can have relevance in Cameroon, Africa and other parts of the world.

Tala takes the debate further when he states that:

> While acknowledging the fact that there is considerable potential for an overlap between the three basic forms of oral narratives, the problemof

categorising them still remains. In an attempt to resolve the problem, we intend to emphasise the interplay of fact and fiction within a specific tale. Thus when a tale gets close to true history or real life but at the same time acquires a fictive coloration in the course of transmission, it can be termed a legend. In other words, a legend is made up of a combination of fact and fiction. When there is a greater tendency towards fact, it becomes a "historical legend" and when the greater tendency is toward fiction, it becomes a "romantic" or "mythic" legend. (74)

An example of one of the tales collected from the grass fields of the North West region of Cameroon is *How the Bafut Fought a War against Themselves*. This tale may be located within a historical time frame which is during the pre-colonial period when inter-tribal wars were rife between tribes, caused by land disputes and at times merely for show of force. But there is a great tendency towards fiction as the events unfold. This is generally because over the years, in the process of transmission, different narrators and storytellers have brought in different elements to make the tale more dramatic and equally more interesting as required by the audience's expectations and state of mind. According to Craig Tapping(1990), a good storyteller could tell the same story over and over and it would be fresh in the mind of the listener. He adds that he could even tell the story told by someone else making it more alive and more dramatic by a play of words and inflexion of voices to effect different tones. Today this tale can be categorised as a fable since it is mostly told for entertainment. Though set in Bafut, the tale appeals to many in communities where the quest for power and bravery can be blinding and detrimental to those in blind quests of supremacy. In essence, it transmits the message that while trying to conquer your enemy, you may be indirectly destroying your own kith and kin.

Stith Thompson (1946) states that although the term 'folktale' is often used in English to refer to the "household tale" or "fairy tale" (the German Marchen), such as "Cinderella" or "Snow White", it is also employed in a much broader sense to include all forms of prose narrative, written or oral, which have come to be handed down through the years. He adds that what is important here is the traditional nature of the material which is contrasted to the modern story writers striving for originality of plot and treatment. According to him, the storyteller of a folktale is proud of his ability to hand on what he has received and his desire to impress his readers or hearers with the fact that he is bringing something that has the stamp of grid authority of a great storyteller or from some aged person who remembered it from old days.

Thompson also affirms that it is impossible to make a complete separation of the written and oral traditions. He justifies this on the grounds that their interrelation is so close and so inextricable as to present one of the most difficult problems the folklore scholar faces, because they differ in their behaviour but are alike in their disregard of originality of plot and of pride of authorship. He adds that we should realize that stories have frequently been taken down from the lips of uneducated "tale tellers" and have been written in the great literary collections. He adds that a story is frequently taken from the people, recorded in a literary document, carried across continents or preserved through centuries, and then retold to a humble entertainer, who adds it to their repertory. In a bid to fixate the role of the oral art, Thompson affirms:

> *Stories may differ in subject from place to place, the conditions and purposes of tale telling may change as we move from land to land or from century to century and yet everywhere it ministers to the same basic social and individual needs. The call for entertainment to fill in the hours of leisure has found most people very limited in their resources, and except where modern urban civilization has penetrated deeply they have found the telling of stories one of the most satisfying of pastimes. Curiosity about the past has always brought eager listeners to tales of the long ago which supply the history of his folk. Legends grow with the telling, and often a great heroic past evolves to gratify verity and tribal pride. Religion also has played a mighty role everywhere in the encouragement of the narrative art for the religious mind has tried to understand beginnings and for ages has told stories of ancient days and sacred beings. Often whole cosmologic have unfolded themselves in these legends, and hierarchies of gods and heroes. (6-7)*

According to Taiwo (1967), "folk-tales" are the most popular and the most important form of oral literature that deserves much attention. He states that they deal with situations with which the listeners are familiar or recall some ancient customs like old forms of inheritance or primitive birth and marriage customs. According to Taiwo, much of the ethical teaching a child received used to come from folklore, which remains predominantly didactic and moralistic in nature. He adds that most of the time, the tales are made to have happy endings and involve triumph over difficulties with or without supernatural help. He also observes that in order to understand the culture of any part of Africa, one must read or listen to the folktales because they illustrate the simplicity and superstition of the rural African peoples, reflect the stage of development of a particular society, reveal the fierce sense of justice of Africans, their belief in witchcraft, and their powers of patience and endurance. Taiwo identifies five different kinds of folktales. Firstly, tales of demon lovers with magic in them, in which the gods take part in the love affairs of men or in which there is some sort of magical intervention or uncanny coincidence to bring about a happy or unhappy ending; the Why stories, moralistic fables, told to pass across some important moral ideas or lessons; fertility tales, which are concerned with the desperate attempts by women to have children and cease to be an object of ridicule in their society, and the trickster tales, which have something to do with the tortoise, endowed with great cleverness; riddles which embody the wisdom and doubts of a race, and which reflect the people's basic concerns and interests. Story-telling sessions start with riddles to alert the minds of the children, and proverbs which emphasise the words of the wise and are the stock-in-trade of old people, who use them to convey precise moral lessons, warnings and advice, since they make a greater impact on the mind than ordinary words. On this note Wolfgang Merder (1987) states that folklore studies should now not swing to the other extreme and merely deal with the innovative survival of texts in the world of popular culture and mass media. The historical and cultural aspects of traditional materials, he intimates, must play a serious role in folklore scholarship. Folklore, according to Merder, at its best addresses both tradition and innovation and shows how constancy and change are interlined in the dynamic process of civilization. Merder from the aforementioned benefits raises the following issues worth examining as far as redynamisation is concerned. These include the demands of new social environments, the role of new variations and innovation of folklore, the demands of adaptation and new uses and functions of folklore and cautions on over-reliance on innovation. It is on this vein that William Bascom (1976) considers folklore, an all-inclusive term, as a bridge between literate and non-literate societies. He goes further to state that:

> *Since folklore serves to sanction and validate religious, social, political and economic institutions and to play an important role as an educative device in their transmission from one generation to another, there can be no thorough analysis of any of these other parts of culture which does not give serious consideration to folklore.(26)*

He also adds that folklore is part of man's learned traditions and customs and a part of social heritage. On this note Alembong reminds us of the sacred values of folklore by intimating that funeral celebrations in traditional "Nweh" society do not seem to project the entertainment aspect of folklore to the fore but emphasise on the mystical, spiritual, the validation of culture and the expression of socially approved norms.

Our focus in this study is on the oral tale of the peoples of the grassfield and forests of the North West and South West Regions of Cameroon. In the process of transforming the tale into play, the tale collected will have to undergo some modifications. The dramatist or play narrator will be expected, in the words of Bascom, *'to modify a well-known tale by the substitution of new characters or incidents in an original way or the introduction of a novel twist to the plot'* *(29)*. Aspects of setting and dialogue can also be modified in the process. The final product, based on the original tale now lends itself to the evaluation meant for stage, movies and cartoons once more adopt a new posture destined for a modern folk and theatre audience. It is in this respect that Bascom states that folklore does not differ from the graphic and plastic arts, music, or dance, where creativity on the part of the performer may be expected.

The oral tale is another important component of the storytelling event, which determines the mood and outcome of the storytelling process. A successful and well-narrated tale leaves the audience and the narrator beaming with delight and pride while a poor rendition of the same tale may lead to dissatisfaction and even conflict. The oral tale dominates storytelling events in the villages and rural areas of Cameroon and Africa. The prose narratives which are written versions of oral tales dominate the audiences in urban centres and cities of Africa where there is a reading and information culture backed by modern forms of communication like the radio, television and internet. Tala, drawing from the characteristics provided by Chukwuma, examines the tale as being fictional and secular, transmitted by the personal word of mouth and can only exist when realised in an oral communicative process. The tale in its prose or written form, apart from being told orally can also be transmitted through a textbook, radio, film and television programmes, a classroom lesson and Internet facilities. In this present age of a global village, transmission and preservation of oral and prose narratives also resides in the hands of writers, musicians, poets, play and film writers and producers and cartoonists. Providing a definition of the storytelling event follows a simple analysis of what storytelling is all about. Storytelling is the act of telling stories as a means of communicating past and current events about people, places and incidents in a given community. The storytelling event is part of an integral study of traditional African literature. Considered as Orature and Oral literature by some critics, the storytelling event combines textual and extra-textual features in the process of narrating African tales, poetry, songs and panegyric.

The oral tale cannot be complete without the context in which it evolves. This context is what has been considered the storytelling event. Paul Mbangwana (1983) defines the storytelling process as a form of communication that carries a message that is encoded and transmitted on the one hand and decoded and received on the other. These activities are realised by the performer and the audience or the "storyteller" and the "story-listeners". Mbangwana goes on to state that: *"Audience participation affects the form and content of the tale more than the verbal text of the tale, which has always been considered by philologists as the sole text, which expresses only one of the many complex aspects of the tale (105).* According to him, the narrator on the other hand, may embellish, recast and refine stories so that they bear the mark of his creative genius or come out with new tales based on his daily experiences. He cites the following feedback and reinforcements as the storyteller composes his tale in front of a participatory audience. These include heated arguments, debates and protests that may end the tale abruptly; a series of interrogations, ponderings and remarks from the audience to direct or shape the plot; whisperings as signs of bewilderment or scepticism, and exclamations and applause at the end to vent their emotions. He goes ahead to state that the audience may show smiles on their faces with no audible word; they may nod, clap and shrug their shoulders; they may join the narrator to end the tale and may also take part in singing and dancing. These explanations suit storytelling in a rural setting which is fast losing a foothold in the urban and semi-urban areas of Africa.

In order to understand the social context of the oral tale within the context of globalisation, it will be important to paint a vivid picture of storytelling in a traditional setting, especially in the villages and semi-urban areas where the storytelling tradition is still vibrant. It is also important to analyse storytelling in a modern setting. This includes urban villages, towns and cities in Cameroon and Africa where modern forms of communication and entertainment are in vogue. These portraits seek to situate storytelling caught in between two worlds separated by a tiny chord, which is moving towards an imminent merger of rural and urban settings.

The Storytelling Event

Storytelling events are forums grouping people from individual homes, villages and communities with the aim of interacting, communicating and sharing certain values, mores and traditions that influence the individual and collective growth and development of people in a community. It involves the interaction of two or more people sharing certain linguistic, ethnic and cultural realities. The outcome of this interaction is to educate, moralise, entertain and hand down certain values to the younger generations. An individual or group of people may play the role of narrator (s) or storyteller (s) while another group, the audience or listener. The storyteller and listener operate under special and prescribed rules of their community or village. They are not allowed to go against these rules; for when they do the sanctions range from outright stripping of titles and other advantages to an invitation of a curse. In a modern setting, prizes are lost and participation for future events cancelled.

The storyteller and listener exhibit certain social functions that explain the roles and functions of certain individuals in the community. Tala (1999) points out aspects of social structure which include justifying or reinforcing kinship groupings, exhibiting distinctions of social class, supporting claims to particular social functions and providing a rationale for social continuities or changes. He also goes ahead to state that every storytelling event is unique occurring only once in time and space, generating unique systems of social and psychological forces. All these aspects are given impetus and particular importance based on the realities of individual communities and groups.

<u>The Oral Tale Narrator</u>

An important component of the storytelling event is the narrator or storyteller. Two people or an individual may play this role successfully. A narrator may introduce the storyteller by revealing his age, status, great exploits and other merits to the audience. In a second instance the storyteller may introduce himself and levy all merits and praises recognised by the audience. In a third instance, the audience recounts the merits of the storyteller in unison as he mounts the front space. One of the qualities of the storyteller is that he should be open-minded and ready to accept all criticisms that will be levied on him. He should be aware of the age, interests and weaknesses of the audience in front of him. As he meets the needs and aspirations of the audience, he must be careful not to hurt their feelings. He should also be able to improvise and improve upon previous performances.

Mastery of the language and other linguistic codes of the language community is a determinant factor of a successful rendition of a tale. He should have a mastery of the signs and lexical items of the language. He should also have a rich repertoire of the proverbs, idioms and slang of his language community. His intelligence to knead these aspects into a complete linguistic whole will make him consistent and accurate in his art. His mastery of the various gestures and mimetic qualities of particular characters in the tale and his ability to invent, modify and amplify certain characters and situations will earn him more praises and admiration from the audience and the community in general. He should also employ his imagination to alter certain aspects of the plot to suit changing cultural and group realities. A storyteller today will have to adjust to changing socio-cultural and political realities in Africa and the world at large. His dressing and voice-tone should correlate with his status and social class.

The Audience

Another important element of the storytelling event is the audience. The success of any storytelling session is determined by the contributions made by the audience to the storyteller. The audience is also determined by age and other social functions. It may comprise youths, women, men, children or a combination of all. They respond to the message being handed to them by the storyteller. They may be emotional, calm, or agitated based on the tale or experiences shared. The mental or psychological state of the audience will determine the continuity, adjustments and termination of the tale. Once the narrator introduces a song, the audience participates by providing the chorus. This exercise reduces tension and enlivens the audience to continue the process of narrating the tale. Verbal exchanges on the part of the audience are based on rules governing storytelling in the particular community. Members of the audience pose questions to the narrator who provides answers without hurting the feelings of the audience. Feedback provided by the audience determines the success or failure of the tale. Views shared by the audience, no matter how childish, critical, or mundane contribute to the success or failure of the storytelling process. Such feedback and reinforcements, as proposed by Mbangwana, include heated arguments, debates and protest if the tale ends abruptly or if the plot lacks logic and if undue punishment is given to one of the characters. Another reaction comprises interrogations, ponderings and remarks when certain parts of the story are obscure or when there is complete ignorance of certain things mentioned in the tale. The audience may whisper in order to crack a joke or to show their bewilderment and scepticism. Also, there are spontaneous exclamations when the audience is moved by fear, fright, surprise, astonishment and disgust. The audience may also applaud, beam with delight and respond by nodding, clapping, shrugging at exciting moments of the performance. The narrator and audience may jointly end the tale and extend ideas unrelated to the story. Members of the audience versed with the language of the tale may complete or clarify some elliptical clauses or ideas expressed as the tale is being narrated. Finally, the audience may join the narrator to sing and dance at the end of a successful tale.

A major category of a storyteller is a textbook writer or novelist. He collects stories from their original settings and transcribes them. He edits and transforms them into a text of his choice. He may publish them in a magazine, a text that contains collection of tales or in a reader for primary and secondary schools. Tales for a reader are usually rendered more accessible if the authors add pictures, drawings, illustrations and questions to stimulate the minds of his readers or audience. Agnes Nzuh is one of those who can pass for a modern storyteller as she has successfully used her knowledge in pedagogy to write some tales with a bearing to the grassland and forest of Cameroon that have moral significance to students in Cameroon secondary schools. She included picture illustrations, drawings and questions to make the process of learning and acquisition easier and faster. The relatively short stories motivate the students to read on. Under this category are novelists who make use of tales to fit into the experience of the characters in the novel. Tala observes how modern writers like Chinua Achebe, Joseph Ngongwikuo, Kenjo Jumban, Ngugi Wa Thiongo and Wole Soyinka have transferred oral literary pieces into written literature. These writers play the role of creative storytellers as they merge human stories with other aspects of their cultural landscape to come out with long fascinating series of episodes and experiences. The audience who is distant can sit in his or her room to listen to the tale as it is being narrated through a written text. This text replaces the human storyteller who is strange in the minds of the audience and seen only through the first or third person narrative technique.

This textbook narrator has come to be admired by the urban audience more than a local storyteller. He is richer, more socially and politically influential than his counterpart in the village. He lives in luxury and is regarded as a scholar par excellence. In some places, he has been awarded with honorary academic degrees even when his mastery of the necessary theoretical and critical approaches is wanting.

PART THREE

Background, Methodological and Theoretical Standpoints

Geographical Background

According to the Central Bureau of Census and Population Studies (BUCREP) Cameroon's population as of 2010 stood at nineteen million, four hundred and six thousand, one hundred (19.406.100) inhabitants based the 2005 demographic census. Recent statistics by *Countrymeters* reveal that as of 1 January 2015, the population of Cameroon was estimated to be twenty-three million, one hundred and nine thousand, eight hundred and seventy-one people. Cameroon occupies a single and unique position in Africa as it is a bridge between Central Africa and West Africa, humid Africa and arid Africa, and French speaking and English speaking Africa. Bordered by the West by Nigeria, to the East by Chad and the Central Africa Republic, to the North by Lake Chad, and to the South by Congo Brazzaville, Gabon, Equatorial Guinea and opening into the Atlantic Ocean. A vast majority of the population is concentrated on the Northern and Western Highlands.

The South West Region, where part of this research was carried out, is bordered to the south by the Atlantic Ocean; to the north by the North West Region; to the East by the Littoral and Western Regions and to the west by the Federal Republic of Nigeria. It is divided into six divisions which include Ndian, Manyu, Kupe-Muanenguba, Meme, Fako and Lebialem. According to the 2005 census, it has a population of 1,384,286 inhabitants covering an area of 25,410 km2 (9,811 sq m). Buea is the capital situated at the foot of Mount Fako. The dense forest areas of the region are found in Ndian, Manyu, Meme and Kupe-Muanenguba where the rural populations are interested in farming, hunting, and petty trading with goods mainly from Nigeria. They plant food crops such as cocoyams, cassava, plantains, banana, maize, beans and yams and cash crops such as cocoa, rubber, palms and coffee.

The North West Region is bordered to the south by the South West Region, to the east by the West Region and the Adamawa Regions and to the west and north by the Federal Republic of Nigeria. It is made up of seven divisions which include Boyo, Bui, Donga-Mantung, Menchum, Mezam, Momo and Ngo-Ketunjia. According to the 2005 census, its population stands at 1,804,695 inhabitants, with Bamenda as headquarters. By 2010 its population was estimated at 1.8 million. The grass field region is made up of the Northern and Western highlands. The Northern Highlands which include the North, Adamawa and Far North Regions is made up of a group of semi-nomadic herdsmen of Choa-Arabs, Kotoko, Massa Toupouri and Mousgoun found mostly in the North. In the Northern mountains are the Kanouri and Kirdi. At the plateau are mainly the Bororo herdsmen. On the Western grass field mountains are found the Semi-Bantus with the Bamilekes and the Bamouns forming the largest of these groups. On the North-Western mountains are the Makon, Bali, Bafut, Kom, Nso, and Oku. The main occupations of the people of the grass field are farming, hunting, trading, carving, fabric manufacturing, and sculpture.

The grass field groups, according to Michaela Pelican (2006, p.39), form a cultural unit organized in more or less hierarchical chiefdoms and confederations with a variety of political institutions, with Bafut, Bali-Nyonga, Kom, Mankon, Nkwen and Nso being the largest and most prominent chiefdoms. Michaela also points to many smaller polities which include the Nchaney and Bessa who are the indigenous or local population group of the Misaje area. Pelican also points out that the people share common ancestral beliefs that are significant in the groups' self- understanding and socio-political organization, and that a majority of Grass fielders are farmers who plant crops such as cereals, tubers, plantains, pulses, gourds, greens, vegetables, fruits, sugar cane, kola nuts, oil palms and coffee. They are also involved in animal husbandry such as the rearing of cattle, chicken, goats, sheep and pigs. Another characteristic which identifies them is linguistic diversity. On this note he quotes Gordon (2005: 56-74), who states that in the whole of Cameroon more than 280 language groups have been identified, with the highest concentration in the Western grass fields with about seventy language groups. He also points out that the Cameroon Grass fields are generally characterized by a high degree of mobility and internal migration. He refers to Nkwi (1987), and Warnier (1987), who pointed out that in the pre-colonial period, mobility was encouraged by "inter-chiefdom" relations and individual participation in a complex system of short and long-distance trade. He cites Boutrais (1995/96:216-217) who states that they are located on the Western Highlands, at an altitude of 10000 to 3.000 metres. The landscape, he intimates, is varied and includes mountain ranges, grass- covered plateaus, wooded valleys, plains, volcanic lakes and many rivers. Due to high altitude, the Grass field region has a pleasant climate with an annual rainfall of 2.000mm and a moderate dry season that lasts from November to March. He also cites Boutrais (1995/96:235-270), who points to the fertile soil due to its volcanic origins. According to Paul Nchoji Nkwi (1989), the present North West Region and most of the western Region of Cameroon came to be known as the Grass fields or Grasslands at the dawn of German penetration of the North West Region. He intimates that its beautiful meadows and grassy hills and mountains could be seen for miles characterized by exposed ridge and unfrosted rocky slopes and forest galleries along the river valleys. He also points out that early travellers to the region were usually impressed by the beautiful grassy landscapes which are today punctuated by new types of trees (Eucalyptus) and the sparkling zinc roofs that could be seen for miles.

Brief Political Climate

The political climate of the forest and grass fields of Cameroon is characterized by multi-party democracy. The CPDM has a stronghold in the forest regions as revealed by recent presidential, parliamentary and council elections, while a few opposition parties share the grass fields of Cameroon with the Cameroon People's Democratic Movement(C.P.D.M)which is making aggressive steps towards complete dominance. Cameroon is divided into ten administrative regions and D.O.s, Gendarmes and police are weapons used to guarantee peace and security. The Union of the Peoples of Cameroon (U.P.C) still occupies a few bastions of the South West and North West Regions. In the Western grass fields, the Cameroon Democratic Union (C.D.U) and the Social Democratic Front (S.D.F) continue to animate the political arena.

<u>Economy</u>

Agriculture, petroleum and forestry remain the main sources of revenue in the forests and grass field of Cameroon. The favourable soils and climatic conditions encourage the growing of cash crops like cocoa, coffee, cotton, rubber, tobacco, tea, pepper, pineapple, palms, groundnuts, millet, and food crops like plantains, coco-yams, rice, beans, yams, cassava, banana, etc. Fishing is carried out mainly in the coastal regions of the South West Region both in small and commercial quantities. Crude oil exploitation is currently going on in the coastal region of the forest inland, especially around the Bakassi Peninsula, while in the grass field, there is the extraction of other mineral resources like iron ore, bauxite, and diamond ore.

<u>Field Methodology</u>

This section dwells on the different fieldwork techniques which we employed in data collection, establishing a rapport between the informants and the researcher, and in evaluation, interpretation and analysis. This study would not have been realised without fieldwork based on observation, interview and administration of questionnaires in the process of data collection and analyses based on practical storytelling activities. It is important to note that the fieldwork exercise was motivated by the absence of a tradition of storytelling in urban and semi-urban settings, the lack of data on the oral tale due to a paucity of research in the area, and the gradual disappearance of narrators and storytellers due to ill-health and death. The desire therefore to contribute to the process of data collection, preservation and propagation via recent forms of communication and information technology motivated me to embark on a search for tales that could be adapted to meet the objectives of this study. Guided by lectures and research on orature in the Department of African Literature and Civilizations in the University of Yaoundé I, especially debates on oral literature in the era of globalisation animated by Professor Binam Bikoi and Professor Nol Alembong; lectures I delivered to students in the Performing and Visual Arts Unit in the Department of English in the University of Buea on drama, research on film script writing, film and comic strips carried out in the Department of Arts and Archaeology in the University of Yaoundé I , and in Essen-Duisburg University in Germany, and Library and Internet research in the University of Buea Library and IT Centres, I was set for fieldwork, data collection, analyses and practical demonstration. I therefore set out with a voice cassette recorder equipped with a built-in microphone, questionnaires, a note-book, warm clothing, leather sports shoes, some money for transportation and lodging and gifts for the elders, traditional leaders, children and other people I hoped to meet and interview.

The technique of observation was useful in ascertaining that the selected areas for fieldwork led me to the desiredsources of information and data relevant to the set goals, objectives and results. The observation methods, according to Kenneth Goldstein (1964), are "those methods used by the field worker in obtaining data by direct observation, looking from the outside in and describing the situation as he sees it". A host of observation methods exists which the observer can employ to obtain relevant data and information.

The field worker can pose as a participant observer which entails the direct observation of the actual context. According to Goldstein, he may either play the role of an active participant in the situation to be observed or pose as a mere onlooker or inactive participant. As an active participant, he is in a vantage position to observe with other participants in order to identify and obtain information on the internal content of the situation instead of only its mechanics. On the other hand, he may simply play the role of an onlooker or inactive participant wherein he remains on the fringe of the action and notes the mechanics of the event. Goldstein points out that there exist two types of contexts in which folklore exist or is performed. These include the natural folklore context and the artificial folklore context. The observer can operate in both contexts to obtain useful data or information.

The natural context according to Goldstein is the social context in which folklore actually functions in a society. On this note he identifies the *highly formal context,* the *semi-formal* and *informal contexts.* The *highly formal context,* according to Goldstein, includes activities performed on special occasions such as births, deaths and weddings, or at specific times of the year such as Christmas and New Year. He also points to the *semi-formal context* in which folklore performance or statement is expected, but not required. In this wise he provides the example of parents telling their children tales before bed time or a father reciting riddles to his child for educational purposes. The *informal context* according to him are those in which folklore is performed incidentally or casually, and in which such performance is not required, is unscheduled and usually unexpected. On this note he provides the example of an individual reciting a proverb in the course of conversation, or a barber telling a joke to his barber while getting a haircut or a farmer reciting a weather-prognostication rhyme to a neighbour as the sun sets.

Secondly, Goldstein points to the artificial context in which folklore is performed or organised based on a schedule and natural agreement of the collector and his informants. On this note, Goldstein observes that the intrusion of the collector into a folklore context changes the situation to one in which the actions and performances of the participant become self-conscious to some degree. The artificial context is usually void of spontaneity common in the natural context. His presence will deter him from obtaining useful data which participants take for granted because they are conscious that some keen and strange observer is in their midst. In essence the performers do not do what they actually do but what they say they do. According to Goldstein the artificial context places fewer restrictions on the collector-observer since the time and place of the context are of common knowledge to both the observer and his informants. He points out that storytelling and singing contexts in which only one or two performers and a small family audience are involved can usually be duplicated but larger functions cannot.

Thirdly, the *induced natural context*, according to Goldstein, entails that a collector induces or creates the natural context through the method of *natural context induction* which requires the collector to determine what the natural context or contexts are for the performance of any specific genre of folklore in the community in which he is doing his field work. The next stage is for him to find an assistant or, where the situation permits, be the instigator himself. This person should be a performer who had taken part in a natural context. His role is to assemble his relatives and friends for an evening of storytelling, singing, riddling or any other activity normally performed in such a context. In this wise Goldstein cautions that the collector must operate with little fanfare as possible and without informing the participants that the purpose of the session is to allow a collector to observe them in action. This can be achieved if the collector has established an excellent relationship with his informants and spent sufficient time socialising with them on occasions. Based on the aforementioned, Goldstein states that the collector may observe the physical setting, the social setting, interaction between participants, performance, time and duration, sentiments expressed, miscellaneous observation and the observer.

The *induced natural context* was useful during the process of observation. It made it possible for me to enlist the assistance of informants who are familiar with the natural context of storytelling and also to socialise with them and members of their families. Although they were conscious of the fact that there was a stranger in their midst, this did not deter them from putting in their best during the storytelling process. Such an atmosphere of collegiality enabled me to observe and record the tales without any distraction on the part of the observers.

As a researcher and collector, I made sure I was adequately equipped for the field. This entail that I was in possession of a note book, pens, pencils, an audio recorder, a laptop computer, a bag and proper clothing and shoes to withstand the cold weather and rugged terrain especially during the rainy season in parts of the North West and South West Regions. With the assistance of relevant information on the different research areas, and with the aid of research guides on the field, I set out to meet the informants, establish a rapport with them, and to begin collecting the necessary data and information. With the aid of the guide, I had an indication of where, when and with whom some items of the folklore existed. In Bafut, for example it was with the aid of the fon's secretary that I was led to my main informant, Nsuh Francis Tumesang of Funtah-Mbeba who not only narrated the tales in the presence of his wife and children, but granted me an interview based on guided questions. It was also with the assistance of Daniel Asongwe, a prince and one of the notables of Ntingkag-Mankon that I was granted audience with Fon Angwafor III. Most of the stories were narrated in English since a majority of my informants spoke and understand English. After the recording, I replayed the tape on the recorder with the aid of an earphone and with the aid of a pen, wrote down the tales as narrated during the storytelling sessions. At the end of the day, I typed the tale with my laptop computer and with the aid of a dictionary, I verified the spellings and meanings of difficult words and expressions. As an adapting artist and literary aesthetician, I was interested in the complete tale as told by the teller in order to make my aesthetic evaluations and to identify the various aspects that would be relevant in the process of adaptation. This set the pace for the utilisation of the interview method.

The interview method was also used to obtain vital information and data related to the study. According to Goldstein interviewing is the most common fieldwork method employed by folklore collectors. He points out that interview method supplies the collector with an insider's view to the individual, his culture and his folklore. Goldstein points to two types of interview methods relevant to folklore research: the *non-directive interview* method and the *directive interview* method. The former, according to Goldstein, "contains a rather generalised conversation between a collector and his informant in which the informant is allowed almost completely free rein after the collector has suggested a subject"(p.108). In this vein Goldstein intimates that the collected is expected to allow his informant talking without disturbing his thought processes and without influencing the informant's behaviour or statements by comments or by the force of the collector's personality. The *directive method* on the other hand entails that the collector elicits highly specific information on particular subjects, ideas and materials. On this note Goldstein propose that it is better to prepare specific questions in advance, with each question ordered to set up a frame of reference for succeeding questions enabled me to get an insider's view of my informant, his culture and other relevant data such as his name, age, residence, occupation, and where, when and from whom he obtained the materials which he is passing on to the collector. My informants include the villagers who narrated the tales, important personalities such as fons and chiefs, village elders, a playwright and experts in creative writing, a film producer/director, teachers, and a comic strip artist.

In order to obtain relevant data and information for this study, I employed the *non-directive interview* method and the *directive interview* method. The former enabled me to obtain general information about the informant, the village, the culture and traditions and the tales, while the latter enabled me to get specific and important information with the aid of a pointed series of questions. On this note, I ensured that the questions were not read out directly but in a conversational tone without the aid of notes. At certain intervals, I endeavoured to be flexible by re-ordering the questions when necessary and omitting some of them completely. In essence I shuttled between the two interview techniques. With the aid of a sound recorder, I was able to collect the details of the conversation through a playback of the recording. It is also worth noting that the interviews were carried in both an audience and non-audience contexts. The tales were all narrated in the presence of the narrators, some members of their family, neighbours and friends. Expert interviews on specific issues concerning the role and place of the oral tale and other important issues on adaptation were carried in non-audience contexts. At the end of each interview exercise, I transcribed recorded interviews to paper, the data later keyed into my laptop computer and the tape kept in a warm and safe place.

The use of the questionnaire also proved useful in the process of data collection. Goldstein states that the questionnaire has the ability to obtain information in depth from a distance on almost every form of folklore subject without having to send out trained field workers to conduct personal interviews. They are fast means of obtaining information without the active presence and participation of collectors. . The administration of well-designed questionnaires enabled this researcher to obtain information from different groups and members of the society about the oral tale, its place and importance and the different avenues open to its redynamisation and modernisation. Guided by specific questions, the respondents provided varied responses depending on their age, knowledge and experience of the socio-cultural landscape of the area of research and the raison d'être of redynamising the oral tale in an era of globalisation.

In the light of the above, a written questionnaire was designed, structured and directed towards children and youths between 9 and 30 years of age. Eleven questionnaires were directed to those between 31-40 and six to those between the ages of 40 and 48 to get some contrary views to those who lived the storytelling event in the past and are now engulfed by new western forms of communication and entertainment. Respondents' names were not included but their ages, status, place of residence and ethnic group were taken into consideration. In all, 120 questionnaires were filled. Those between the ages of 9 and 14 filled 14, those between 15 and 20 filled 36 and those between 21 and 25 filled 34 questionnaires. To support the focus to our study, 65 suggested that the tales be transformed into plays, movies, comic strips and cartoons; 20 suggested that the tales be taught in primary and secondary schools, 8 held the opinion that people should be trained at local and national levels as professional storytellers, 23 intimated that parents should allocate time in the evening to tell stories to their children. As a point of concern, 35 out of 65 between the ages of 9 and 20 preferred cartoons. This shows the interest placed by the young in this form of entertainment, which could convey all the moral, educational, and socialising values of the African prose narratives.

With the aid of the performance context approach to theatrical analysis, the tale was narrated with the aid of Process Drama carried out amongst students in Form Three in Government Secondary School, Bwiyuku and in the University of Buea amongst undergraduate students of the Performing and Visual Arts Students and students from Bloomsburg University in the United States of America.

As far as fieldwork proper is concerned, my trip to the forest regions of the South West Region extended from the mountain village of Bokwango in Buea, the Paramount Chief's Palace in Buea, the palace of the Chief of Banga-Bakundu in Mbonge Sub-Division, the Bafaw village in Kumba Central Sub-Division, to Tombel and Nkack-Muasundem in the Kupe and Muanenguba Division. Findings from the field were different and varied depending on the social status, age, profession and world view of the person interviewed.

A majority acknowledged having forgotten most of the tales learnt while growing up. Most of the narrators could not give a complete rendition of a tale without breaks and intervention of other participants. I discovered that there was a general breakdown in communication between parents and children because of the presence of the television in most homes and compounds. A majority of those interviewed acknowledged the absence of storytelling in their homes and localities. They also saw the need for the act of storytelling to be revived in all its forms. They were unanimous on the introduction of storytelling in the school curriculum and the transformation of tales into cartoons for children's textbooks and comic strips for the television. There existed different versions of a particular tale with animal stories forming a majority of tales collected.

In the North West Region, my trip began from Ntingkag in the Mankon Fon's Palace in Bamenda to Mbebali near the Bafut Fon's Palace, Bawok in Bali and Bamessing in Ndop. My findings reveal the following: firstly, the grassfield regions of the North West are strongly linked by strong and unified chieftains characterized by the respect of traditional rulers and institutions. Those interviewed also acknowledged a downward trend in the story-telling event and the slow disappearance of the tales in the face of modern technology and communication. They unanimously hold the view that the story-telling event can be revived if the fons and traditional elders call on their subjects to tell stories in their individual homes and village groupings. Pa Limen Peter, for example, suggested that the Fon should instruct each quarter head and notable to form committees to revive this aspect of the culture. He affirmed that if the fons play this role, there will be reason for hope.

Most of the stories in the North West were myths and legends that explained the creation of institutions, existence of supernatural beings and the exploits of great men during wars and tribal conflicts. Most of the informants affirmed that with the availability of electricity and fuel generators in most villages, most people now own television sets; so transforming the tales into cartoons, especially for television, will strengthen the visual aspects and serve home teaching and entertainment. The Fon of Mankon suggested that school authorities should hire the services of professional storytellers in their respective villages to pass on some of the stories to the pupils and students in primary and secondary schools. He vouched to support the creation of local radio and television houses that have as mission the propagation of the culture of the people. He also advocated for cultural festivals where some of the animal stories and legends could be dramatised.

Data collection in the field was facilitated by a tape-recorder and notebook. My informants did not only lament on the downward trend being experienced by the storytelling event, they provided an opportunity for their tales to be narrated before an audience. This exercise was motivated by Elizabeth Fine (1994, p.68) who intimates that in order to fulfil the theoretical claims about the nature of verbal art as an aesthetic communicative process, the text must record and present its data in a manner which is consistent with the concepts of the performance approach. Fine also affirms that the text must represent the aesthetic mode of performance and warns that if the text represents a performance only as a communicative process, it has failed to capture the essence of the transaction that separates performance from other modes of communication. It is in this same light that Alembong's proposed storytelling traditions were taken into consideration in the textual presentation of the tales. It is important to note that the tales in this study were collected in strict respect of these principles and the practical adaption of the tales into play, film scripts and comic strips endeavour to continue the practicalities of the event. In line with the pre-storytelling event, most of the tales were narrated in the presence of a narrator and an audience who began their tale with a proverb, a riddle and the Arabic tradition of opening. It is not uncommon that most of the tales opened with the following words: "Arabian Nights—"uttered loudly by the Narrator, while the audience or listener responded "entertainment", presented as follows:

a. Narrator: Arabian Nights---?

b. Listener(s) entertainment!

c. Narrator: Are you ready?

d. Listener(s) yes

e. Narrator: Boys and girls, I want to tell you a story!

f. Listener(s): what is your story about?

g. Narrator: My story is about-----

By the end of the process of field data collection, a host of tales were collected. Some of the tales collected include

Yomandene and the Stubborn Son, How the Bafut Fought a War against Themselves, The Death of Leopard and many others. For practical purposes I selected *Yomandene and the Stubborn Son* for adaptation in a formal classroom setting. Prior to the narration, two Bakweri proverbs were told by the narrator before the story. These include: "When you want to punish a dog you do not show it the whip" and "you do not disown your child because he excretes on your legs." Such an exchange prepared the minds of the listeners, freed their minds from any previous distractions and thoughts, and left them alert and attentive to the narrator who now assumed the position of teacher and master.

At the end of the exercise, it was observed that chieftaincy in the South West Region, which suffered from long years of colonial domination and political influence, has affected the respect due traditional authority in many villages of the region. It was also discovered that the terrain is not too hilly although most parts of the roads remain untarred and bumpy, making the movement of cars and persons difficult. On the other hand, penetration into the villages and traditional institutions of the North West Region remain difficult and risky. For example, it took a whole week to see the fon of Bafut, who denied granting any interview and ordered his secretary to lead me to the prominent storytellers of the village.

It was also discovered that the stories from the forest and grass fields of the South West and North West Regions are similar in content and form, but differ slightly from the animal characters mentioned, especially in the case of animal tales. It was also found out that it is difficult to assess the impact of modern forms of communication and entertainment on urban and rural areas because most towns and villages were amalgamating and sharing similar traits and characteristics. It became clear to me that communication is not a problem even in distant areas due to the presence of radio and television signals powered by electrical and fuel generators. Even mobile phone signals are reaching distant and enclave areas thanks to the communication signals being installed by CAMTEL), the Mobile Telecommunication Network(MTN), ORANGE and recently NEXTTEL.

It is worth noting that such an endeavour could not be realized without some setbacks and difficulties. Most of the persons interviewed complained of the impromptu nature of my visit. They suggested that I make a second visit so that they will have ample time to revisit their repertoire of tales, collect many tales and rehearse their rendition. In the North West region, it was difficult to meet traditional leaders. They were also very inquisitive about my mission in their court. Such was the case with the fon of Bafut and the fon of Bali. Most of the persons living around the palace refused to be interviewed except they were certain the researcher had made initial contacts with the Fon. This prolonged my stay in the North West and an increase in my cost of expenditure.

Making a trip to the North West region in the month of August posed great difficulties in accessibility due to the muddy nature of the roads and prolonged rainfall. It was difficult to assess the kinds of tips and gifts that would be appreciated by the persons solicited, so the middle men and interpreters saw my visit as an opportunity to exploit me by exaggerating the fares and prices of certain services and goods in their locality. Due to inadequate funding, the candidate had to borrow money from financial houses on huge interest rates to cover research cost, especially transportation and lodging.

On a general note, my stay and interaction with my informants led me to the conclusion that the abolition of vernacular schools in the then British Southern Cameroons marked a monumental setback in the development of national languages which is now enshrined as a state policy in the 1996 constitution. The abandoning of storytelling in schools and in homes marked the onset of the breakdown in family cohesion, respect of basic societal norms and state institutions. In essence it marked the upsurge of general insecurity, fear, hatred, immorality, and conflicts between individuals, tribes and nations. I also observed that family gatherings and cultural festivals offer an opportunity for stories to be told that serve as moral boosters and aids to social and political cohesion. In essence, storytelling also served as a veritable source of employment, livelihood and financial stability to the professional storyteller and the community that produces the tale. Therefore, reviving the storytelling event either at community or national level will be a great impetus to social cohesion, and economic, cultural and political unity.

At the close of the fieldwork research I observed that the cultural values of unity, solidarity, hospitality and respect of traditions provided healthy grounds for any researcher interested in getting valuable data on any aspect of the history and tradition of these regions. In spite of the poor road network, I realized that accessibility was not a problem since the hospitable nature of the people facilitates the search of reliable and expert informants. I also observed that once an informant was satisfied with the motives of a visit and research, he would go to any length to provide the researcher or the collector with the necessary data or information.

Theoretical Considerations

In order to understand and explain the different dimensions of this work under study, an eclectic approach of analysing and employing Adaptation in theory and practice, Semiotics and New Historicism as a sociological approach will go a long way to blend aspects of form and content that explicate the transformation of the tale to plays, film scripts and comic strips. All these will be employed while exposing present trends in modernisation and production of traditional African literature. Adapting the tales for stage and the audio-visual media will capture the rich and salient features absent from the bare tales. The adaptation process will capture the outline text and supra-text respectively.

Adaptation in Theory and Practice

In this section, adaptation will be examined in line with the performance-context approach that gives life to the oral tale within the context of this research and the process of adaptation will also be applied to the study and practical transformation of selected tale into play.

Firstly, we adapt the tales to meet the demands of a mass audience and their aspirations. When we adapt for stage or screen, for example, we will be addressing an audience of thousands, while a film script writer may be targeting millions, who are disposed but glued to their television screen, laptops and cell phones. In order to fulfil his mission, the script writer must examine the taste and aspirations of the audience, their socio-cultural, historical, economic and political realities. As far as the taste of the audience is concerned, Portnoy intimates that a novel, short story, or play that was written in the 1960s can be updated to appeal to an audience in the 1990s. Apart from this, the taste of those living in urban centres and cities has to be taken into consideration. It is important to note that there is a difference in the taste of city dwellers who are mostly concerned with the acquisition of wealth and appreciating western lifestyles. So, a tale that is adapted for an audience in the rural areas will have to undergo further adaptation to satisfy the taste of the urban audience. As far as the socio-cultural aspects are concerned, there is need for the writer to master and understand the socio-cultural exigencies of the target audience. All of these should be taken into consideration as far as setting, dialogue, characterisation, diction and structure are concerned. With the influence of history, the oral tale can be transformed to accommodate current historical information. With the tales under study the names of characters, be they animal or human must be changed to reflect characters admired and cherished by present day audience. Secondly, the political taste of the writer must be reflected in the story. In this wise, political issues raised in the 1960, will require new answers in 2000.

So, it is important to adapt taking into consideration the recent political demands and atmosphere, especially in an era of globalisation. Thirdly, adaptation protects rich and potential material getting obsolete or extinct. It is important to note that so much literature is lost in libraries, private rooms and book shelves in academic and private circles which have either been used and abandoned, or have never seen the light of day. There are thousands of tales from the different villages and tribes of the ten regions of Cameroon. Some of these tales are either in print form or being handed down by way of mouth from one generation to the next. Scholars and researchers have recorded a host of these tales for their private academic endeavours. Unfortunately, these tales are abandoned as soon as these tasks are completed. As far as narrators are concerned, many of them do not live long to hand over the tales to their siblings who are daily attracted to the television and internet. Adapting the tales for stage and screen will not only meet the aspirations of this new audience but will help in documenting preserving and transmitting the tales from one generation to another, and from one social setting to the next. In an interview with a playwright, George Nyamndi, when posed a question on the benefits of adapting from one literary genre to another affirms:

> *I think the advantages are many, even if they come with creative challenges. The very first one is that to adapt you must first of all be won over by the source genre as it were. In this case the novel. If the novel does not speak to you, you wouldn't go beyond that level of readership attention into that second stage that consists of transforming*

yourself into a vehicle of whatever message the novel intends to send out. Now, in adapting, the tendency is to move from a broader narrative texture to a more concise, immediate streamlined version, in this case drama. So when you adapt you also remove some of the less urgent, some of the less important aspects of the novel's narrative form and you go for a message that is dramatised. Drama is all about dramatizing message, dramatizing issues of immediate importance. So I think that when you adapt, the basic motivation is to make the message more immediate and more available to a wider public. And that way you dramatize not only what the novel says, but the potential effect of what it says on the audience or the reader as the case may be. So there are, as I say, immediate gains, immediate advantages, immediate reasons for wanting to adapt. But the pre-condition for that adaptation is interest in the original document. Because if I had read Things Fall Apart and had not found it worth my while, I wouldn't have bothered going into that second stage of adapting it.(G. Nyamndi, personal communication, February 25,2015).

Adaptation is one of the major instruments of transforming any idea, story or historical narrative. Linda Hutcheon (2003, p39) affirms:

The desire to transfer a story from one medium or one genre to another is neither new nor rare in Western Culture. In fact, it is so common that we might suspect that it is related to how the human imagination creates... Most of Shakespeare's plays were adapted from other literary or historical works but that doesn't seem to have damaged the Bard's reputation. Shakespeare transferred his cultural stories from page to stage and made them accessible to (and enjoyable for) a largely illiterate audience. In recent years, it is true, we have witnessed on our television screens and in our movie theatres enough adaptations – based on everything from comic books to the novels of Jane Austen – to make us wonder if Hollywood has run out of new stories. There must be infinitely more candidates for the Academy Award for the Best Adapted screenplay than there are for the Best Original screenplay. (39)

These claims may appear troublesome to those who believe in originality. Adapters combine creativity and originality to the process of adaption; else the adapted story becomes a photocopy of the original tale. In Africa, the scenario seems to be related to the Western scene as described above by Hutcheon. In order for the adapting artist not be accused of plagiarism or a 'copycat', he must be able to blend his creative talents with his adapting skills.

The new visual, apart from audio or print ,have attracted a wider audience even in local settings, with modern adapters banging on their poetic license, and viewing adaption as the only way out of recreating interesting stories from mouth to print and film. In this wise, stories that used to animate bedtime conversations in the past can still be enjoyed by fanatics of film, television and internet. On this note, Hutcheon (2014) sees adaptation as a formal phenomenon; and a combination of translation and usually distillation of the adapted work. He adds that there is no such thing as a literal adaptation. On this note he postulates that transportation to another medium always means change involving gains and losses. In relation to our study, the original nature of the tales under study can never be compromised. They remain original by way of mouth and the story teller remains the original custodian of the tale. It is usually considered that his death may mean the end of a tale if he has not successfully transferred the tale to a new narrator who may be his son, brother or trusted kinsman.

During a forum held during the XVTH ASSITEJ Congress and General Assembly in Montreal Canada in September 2005 on the topic *"Adapting Literature into Theatre – International Thoughts"*, Luiza Monteiro summarised the topics of the discussion as follows:

1. The differences and similarities between inter-cultural and intracultural adaptations.

2. The difference between editing, adapting, and creating a new piece of art

3. The main difference between and requirements of a piece of literature and a theatrical production.

4. The commercial aspect of adapting children's literature to theatre – we are often tempted to use popular literature because it "sells well".

5. The moral issues in the use of 'diary theatre' – do we have the right to edit and adapt real and personal experiences?

6. Who has ownership of the work and who is the best person to adapt – the original writer or a theatrical practitioner – or a collaboration of both?

7. We should remember that some books are well known and well-liked by children, how much right do we have, therefore, to change them into something totally new?

8. What does the book mean to us now, here, today? What is the underlying trust? What do we take and honour?

These topics are relevant to every adapting artist in the execution of his task and if the end product has to meet the needs of the audience. Hutcheon goes further to state that it is probably safe to say that the intended receiver of the work is on the mind of the adapter from the start. On this note he points out that one of the main issues that raised concern was whether the audience knows the adapted text or is ignorant of it. On this note he affirms that there is more creative freedom for the adapter, but if the text is well known, then there is risk of a palpable tension between the audience's desire for fidelity to the believed literary work and the creator's desire for autonomous reconfiguration or even critical commentary.

Cheela Chilala (2005) outlines two broad types of adaptation: *intra cultural adaptations*–from one art form to another (e.g. book to film, film to radio etc.) within the same culture and *inter cultural adaptations* – from culture to another. Our study falls under 'intra cultural adaptations', with the grass field and forest cultures being diverse tributaries of Cameroonian culture. The focus here is from tale to stage, the audience being either people from the forest or grass fields of Cameroon or a mixture of both. Being people who share similar socio-cultural and political realities, the tales are destined not only to address their visions and world views but to bridge the borders that separate both cultural heritages.He also points to the idea of originality common to both intra and inter cultural adaptations. It is important here to note that adaptation should not be a design to completely erase the originality of the tale under study. While moving from tale to stage, the originality of the original text should be respected; else we are accused of distorting cultural facts to suit our selfish adaptation designs.

Josiane Polidoit on the subject of copyright and performing rights intimates that the tales are part of an intangible cultural heritage intimating that there is need for the community that created the tale to keep the source rights while the performing rights are kept by the playwright or adapting artist. Therefore, the play director or teacher who directs or uses the play as a didactic material on stage and class, respectively, have the duty to acknowledge the contribution of the original story teller and the play adapting artist. A percentage of what is derived from stage performance should therefore be shared between the original creators of the tale, the play adapter and the play production team. One way of compensating the original creators or custodian of the tale is by extending some acts of humanitarian or financial gesture to the locality where the tale originates. This can be in the form of providing bore water wells, especially in areas where water is scarce, providing solar panels in areas where there is no electricity, mosquito nets in areas infested by mosquitoes and renovating the fon's palace.

According to Jeremy Turner (2005), what is of interest to him is not simply adapting literature to stage but the mere creative process of making a new force of art inspired by the original story. It is important to note that the new plays, films and comic strips that will be produced from the original tales follow different creative processes. According to Turner, editing is a starting point, which permits the original tale to be edited in order to find the very essence of the story. This, according to Turner, is then used to create a theatre script, the structure of which is often very different from the structure of the original. He also points out some of the characteristics of the original story which is indirect, reflective and descriptive and whose creative process and relationship with its audience are private. But with theatre productions, he states that they are generally more immediate, progressive and reactive; with creative processes usually collaborative and exhibiting close relationships with a direct and public audience. Therefore, theatre adaptations can serve a wider audience and elicit wider audience participation. Such is usually accomplished either during public stage performances or community theatre, where the audience, be they school pupils or farmers take active part during the production process.

Most play directors and theatre activists have successfully interacted with a wider or specified audience using either Augusto Boal's educational tool, *Theatre of the Oppressed* (TO), which helps the participants to see, analyse and act upon their own oppressions, be they internal or external. This can be realised using Forum Theatre which sees the active participation of the spectator at certain instances of the play; *Invisible theatre*, which is a previously rehearsed play that is performed in a public space without the public knowing that it is a play, with the intention to provoke debate and to clarify a problem with the people who experience it; *Legislative theatre* used to open up a dialogue between citizens and institutional entities so that there is a flow of power between both groups; *Image Theatre* which involves participants moulding and sculpting their own bodies or those of others into individual representation of a particular situation, emotion, idea and then move into a group and reform the images they have created to form a picture or 'image' and *Process Drama* which provides an interactive performance platform for the teacher as participant and students all working and contributing to produce a new text that addresses the topic and learners needs and aspirations.

The stage play can be taken back to the original tale community using the techniques of theatre for development which include identifying the problem, locating the workshop, choosing the participants, preparing logistics and theoretical framework, addressing field behaviour and dress code, not leaving out observation, data collection, classification and analysis. By stating priorities and story creation with the aid of rehearsal, performances, post-performance discussions, post mortem review of methodologies and reports, the minds of the participants can be empowered through the acquisition of information on the law, human rights, women's rights, children rights, civil status, and political rights.

Main Actors of the Adaptation Process

The Oral Artist

Isidore Okpewho (1992) observes that "if there is anything of artistic or literary merit in Africa literature, then those who 'create' and perform this literature could be given the same recognition that we gave to novelists, playwrights and poets. This has not been the case. They are not recognized in spite of their skills and dexterity. In most cases, they are usually recognized and sometimes presented with gifts and tokens from students and researchers in African Literature. Okpewho goes further to recommend training and preparation, which can be informal or formal. With regard to informal training, he proposes that long and continuous stay in an environment where an art is practised enables the person to learn or develop the skill in the art. He is able to perfect this skill when he takes active part in regular practice and performance of the art. This interaction and encounter with expert artists also enable him to attain perfection in the art. The child may learn from his or her parents, grandparents, relatives, friends and other artists closer to him or her. With regard to formal training, Okpewho intimates that formal training in more complex forms of oral literature especially in some forms of ritual poetry and performances involving the accompaniment of music is greatly lacking. In this vein he points out that such training is usually encouraged when the future artist considers it a source of living. With oral narratives, members of the community who have had an opportunity to narrate the tale may consider themselves as skilful narrators. It is important at this junction to distinguish between an artist with informal training and a trained artist. It is common to find storytellers who can barely manage to narrate the story without any formal training. Here they rely on mastery of the story line, the chronological sequence of events, and voice. Their status and role in the community are usually added advantages to attract the audience.

The oral artist who has undergone formal training is not only gifted in voice and mastery of storyline but has a mastery of the use of musical instruments, dance and choreographic skills and employs the use of relevant costumes and props. He is usually identified when he makes his first presence from the way he walks. He is usually attracted by children and youths who flock around him to listen to his tale. He usually does not demand a fee and no one cares to reward him for his talent. Presently, we find a host of trained oral artists who are invited by television houses to take part in children programmes. We hereby recommend that these artists be recognized and classified like their counterparts of other fields of arts.

The Adapting Artist

Another second group of artists are adapting artists who take active part in the creative process of literature. They employ their talents to render the tales more suitable to the audience and their social realities. Okpewho refers to this group of artists as makers. On this note, he intimates that we should be honest enough to accept that the material of a huge portion of oral literature in any community comes from the distant past and that the original authors cannot be accounted for due to the passage of time. The absence of a written and audio- visual tradition in the past made it impossible to ascribe authors to particular tales. So, the tale all along has been considered the collective property of members of the community where the tale is narrated.

But who is the adapting artist? He is the one who listens to a tale and decides consciously that such a tale should be spiced by new elements and characters that render the tale more useful to the present generation of that community. He can change the setting of the tale, add more spaces, introduce new characters, eliminate others and change aspects of plot or story line. The question remains: Is he the new author of the tale? Can he claim ownership of the tale because he introduced new characters? In this present dispensation, is he allowed to state that the tale is an original creation of the people of Bafut, for example, while he remains the adapting artist? In a scenario where the adapting artist completely changes the tale to fit into his context, he may pose as the author. Ola Rotimi, for example, remains the author of *The Gods are Not to Blame* an adaptation of Sophocles *Oedipus the king* although his main role was an adapting artist. Isidore Okpewho (1990) illustrates this with reference to Ruth Finnegan's research among the Limba of Sierra Leone when he states:

In a visit to this ethnic group, Finnegan told the story of the temptation and fall of Adam and Eve to a notable Limba narrator, Karanke Dema. More than two years later, she returned to the same community and Karante, who had meanwhile been telling that story to his Limba audiences, volunteered to retell it to Finnegan. The old Judaic story had undergone considerable metamorphosis and now looked every bit like a normal Limba story in terms of form and content. (30)

This second group of adapting artists can truly be considered as makers. As creators and makers, they stamp a note of originality on the tale, thereby rendering it new and original. In essence, adapting artists are able to get inspiration from a former tale to create a new one that addresses their social realities.

The Performing Artist

In order to get a grasp of the role of the audience as performing artist we must take a look at the performance context. Okpewho states that *"there must be a certain appeal not only in what the performer is saying but in the way it is said (whether in the manner of plain speech or of chanting or singing)* (42). The performing artist can be considered the most creative of the artists. He does not rely on the tale handed to him but engages on a creative process while on stage or in front of an audience. He is usually inspired by the audience in front of him, the event or occasion, the age or social class of the audience, the time at his disposal and the motivation he expects at the end of his performance. According to Okpewho, it is in the examination of performance that we are able to see the real character of oral literature as distinct from written literature. He intimates that it is an art form created in the ward presence of an audience ready to contribute its own quota towards the success of the performance.

The Audience as Artist

The audience can be considered an artist because its members are active in shaping and tracing the course of the event. During some traditional storytelling sessions, the performing artist relies at times on the feedback he gets from a member or members of the audience who are versed with the story or similar versions being narrated. Their contributions are either in the form of comments, praises, songs, the provision of vital information related to the culture, tradition and setting of the tale. The *artist-in-audience*, once conscious that the tale is in the course of mutation for a particular purpose and in response to the needs of a new or different audience, will shape or redirect his or her contribution towards modifying the narrative.

In his introduction, Robert Stam (2005) bases his argument on a film which adapts Susan Orlean's *The Orchid Thief*, a non-fiction account of a flower poacher, named La Roche, played by Chris Cooper, working out of the Florida Everglades. Directed by Spike Jonze and written by Charlie Kaufman, the film is entitled *Adaptation*, which according to Stam is an adaptation and an original screenplay which turns a non-fiction book into a fictional adventure. Stam describes the process through a vivid description of the different actors involved by stating:

> *"We see Susan Orlean at her computer, surrounded by the various sources – encyclopedias, botanical books, histories – that feed into her own text. And we see Charles Kaufman, trying to adapt her book, panicked and sweating before the blank computer screen.'* (2)

On this note, Stam points out that film is a form of writing that borrows from other forms of writing. It is therefore true that we cannot adapt what does not exist. But the question arises: "what do we adapt?" Simply put, we can adapt any story, written or spoken, that is interesting and with elements worth entertaining. In essence, a short story an oral tale can be adapted into a full-blown screenplay. A play or sketch can change its form designed for the stage or life audience to a screenplay destined for a cinema or television audience which is the vogue today.

Our focus in this study cuts across three stages: firstly, it involves recording or collecting selected tales from the forest and grass fields of Cameroon, which addresses the socio-cultural, spiritual, and economic needs of not only the peoples of these regions, but Cameroonians and Africans in general. Our illustrations span the stage play to the screenplay ready for production. All these processes will be elaborated and illustrated with vivid examples of adaption and transformation process.

In an attempt to answer the question," why we adapt and transform", we can say that the stage has evolved from the fireside, open auditoriums, vast fields and seaside, through the proscenium stage, the classroom and show centres to the cinema and video halls, the television and presently, the face to face personal computers powered by CD ROMs, VCDs, DVDs, flash drives and the bare face internet, a finished product of globalisation. Today, chats, conversations, debates and conferences are conveniently delivered with participants sitting in their individual rooms no matter on which part of the globe they find themselves, as long as there is internet connectivity. The story telling event can be organised today in the presence of a virtual audience, no matter in which part of the country or world where they find themselves. Their response and feedback can be made through the internet guided by microphones, loudspeakers, and webcam presently fixed to laptops and monitors of personal computers and/or desktops. Storytelling can therefore attract a wider audience today. In the same vein, films which are adaptations of stories can be viewed on television and internet. Stam adds that if mutation is the means by which the evolutionary process advances, then filmic adaptation can be seen as "mutations" that help the source novel, tale or play to "survive". He raises the following questions:

> *Do not adaptations "adapt to" changing environments and changing tastes, as well as to a new medium, with its distinct industrial demands, commercial pressures, censorship taboos, and aesthetic norms? And are adaptations not a hybrid form like the orchid, the meeting place of different "species?"* (3)

He provides answers to these questions by referring to La Roche who holds that creating a hybrid is like playing the role of God Almighty, and sees the process like giant flower parasites that devour and kill their host tree or sources, "sucking the life" out of their hosts." He states that *"even the metaphor of murder is involved." "We have to kill me,"* the Susan Orlean character says of her adapter, *"before he murders my book."*

From the above we can see the resistance towards adaption. Stams considers this as the roots of a prejudice, blamed on the actor(s) involved in adaptation. According to Stam, critics blame the cinema for disservice to literature, using terms like "infidelity," "betrayal," "deformation," "violation," "bastardization," "vulgarization," and "desecration".

He explains all these as follows:

> *"Infidelity" carries overtones of Victorian prudishness; "betrayal" evokes ethical perfidy; "bastardization" connotes illegitimacy; "deformation" implies aesthetic disgust and monstrosity; "violation" calls to mind sexual violence; "vulgarization" conjures up class degradation; and "desecration" intimates religious sacrilege and blasphemy.* (3)

In the midst of such prejudice, which holds true especially to adapters who sacrifice professionalism in place of materialism and financial gains, there is much gain and profit when adapters engage the process systematically to address the needs of the audience .In this study, we shall illustrate the benefits of adaptation while being faithful to the original tale in question. Such a process will involve avoiding to distort the original plot, avoiding intrusions, words and cliche's that deviate from the original language used in the tale. While staying close to the setting, characters, diction, plot and structure of the tale, the finished product should be identified by the creators and custodians of the origin tale.

In lieu of our study, adaptation is not seen as an attempt to downgrade or minimize the efforts of the original storytellers or successive narrators and custodians of the tales under study. The process of adaptation currently engaged is to render the tale more palpable so that it readily fits into the different media that dominate modern means of communication and entertainment. It is also an attempt to render the tales more useful not only as didactic materials but as interesting material worth viewing in relaxed and stress-free environments, which hitherto were created by the storytelling event organised around the fireside in the distant pasts.

He points to a second source of hostility to adaptation which is presumed rivalry between film and literature. In order to demonstrate this, he refers to an old anecdote which holds that the writer and the filmmaker are travelling in the same boat but both harbour a secret desire to throw the other overboard. According to Stam, *"the inter- art relation is seen as a Darwinian struggle to the death rather than a dialogue offering mutual benefit and cross- fertilization"* (4). On this note ,he adds that *"Adaptation becomes a zero-sum game where film is perceived as the upstart enemy storming the ramparts of literature"*(4).This confirms that there was institutional rivalry between the two media.

He blames the third source of hostility to adaptation to 'iconophobia'. He traces this as far back to the Judaic-Muslim-Protestant prejudice against the visual arts, which prohibited "graven images", explicit in the Second Commandment forbidding the making of idols in the form of anything in heaven above or on earth beneath or in the waters below. He also refers to Baudelaires worry about photography corrupting influence on the arts; to Frederic Jameson, a film-literate theorist, who sees the filmic image as essentially pornographic since it demands that we "stare at the world as though it were a naked body;" and Lacan, who views the films iconic "imaginary signifier," as triumphing over the logos of the symbolic written word of which literature remains the most prestigious form. On this note he laments that *"film and other visual media seem to threaten the collapse of the symbolic order, the erosion of the powers of the literary fathers, patriarchal narrators, and consecrated arts"* (5). Our study takes upon an opposite view because it attempts at enhancing and valorising the views, desires and passions of the original story creators to a generation which seems to be falling apart because they are void of the wisdom and knowledge inherent in the original tales. Using Mel Gibson's *The Passion of the Christ*, an adaptation of the crucifixion story of Christ, Stam states that Gibson proclaims his goal to be complete fidelity and also claimed to have attained it.

Stam further refers to a fourth source of hostility to film and adaptation to cultures rooted in the sacred word of the"religions of the book", and points out that many literatures reject films based on literature; most historians reject films based on history, and some anthropologists reject films based on anthropology. He blames all these on the common current rooted on the "nostalgic exaltation" of the written word as the privileged medium of communication. This hypothesis seems to be dwindling because of the gradual decline of the reading culture in favour of television and motion pictures by recent innovations of communication and information technologies. Even visuals are dominant aspects of books and other teaching aids today. It is on this basis that the visuals are regarded as having an impact even in non-literate communities. This can be seen by the importance placed by members of such communities to the lone television screen.

A fifth sense of hostility, according to Stam, stems from anti-corporeality; and distaste for film as obscene. In a bid to support this view, Stam states that *film offends through its inescapable materiality, it's incarnated fleshly, enacted characters, its real locales and palpable props, its carnality and visceral shocks to the nervous system"* (6). Stam quotes Virginia Wolf, who describes the film spectators" as twentieth-century "savages" whose eyes mindlessly "lick up" the screen" whereas literature is seen on a high plane which is more 'cerebral', 'transensual' and 'out-of-body'. Stam adds that while novels are absorbed through the mind's eye during reading, films directly engage the various senses. Stam also alludes to the cognitive theorists who hold that films have an impact on our stomachs, hearts, and skin. In spite of all these, it is important to use films as shock therapies and as panacea to address some of the social ills plaguing modern day society. The subtle impact of the novel is necessary in more stable communities.

A sixth source of hostility, according to Stam, is what he terms "the myth of facility", which hinges on the assumption that films are easy to produce and pleasurable to watch. This is an assumption which does not hold true today, because of the sophistication and heavy financial and human resources needed to produce a single film. We accept the view by one of Stam's literature professors who points out that it takes no brains to sit down and watch a film, because volumes of language and communication involved in a film necessitates a schooled and learned mind, if not the spectator is left with bare images, actions and incomprehensible sounds. Stam affirms:

> *On the production side, the facility myth ignores the diversified talents and Herculean efforts required actually to make films. On the reception side, it ignores the intense perceptual and conceptual labor-the work of iconic designation, visual deciphering, narrative inference, and construction-interent in film."* (7)

A seventh source of hostility, according to Stam, is a "sublimal form of class prejudice which he considers a socialised form of guilt by association. The cinema is seen as degraded because it keeps a "great unwashed popular mass audience", which prefers the cotton candy of entertainment to the gourmet delights of literature. Such hostility is classicist and obnoxious to the power of this 'popular mass' who though considered vulgar, play an important role in these respective societies. Cinema therefore, feeds them with the knowledge they would otherwise have gotten from the novel, if they were literate.

A last source of hostility is what Stam considers "the charge of parasitism. Film adaptations, according to Stam, are seen as parasitical on literature, because they borrow into the body of the source text and its vitality, seen by Kamilia Elliot as copies of the original. In as much as we appreciate 'pure film', we should also encourage adaptations from novels, and plays that have a positive impact on a wider audience. Our stories, though popular, have a positive impact on the moral, spiritual and socio-economic growth of the people.

The Impact of the Post on Adaptation

It is important to survey some of the views raised by the posts on the basis of adaptation. These views will enable us consider the raison-d'etre of adaptation in the present dispensation. Stam is categorical when he points out:

> *Although intertextuality theory certainly reshaped adaptation studies, other aspects of poststructuralism have not been marshalled in the rethinking of the status and practice of adaptation. Derridean deconstruction, for example, undid overly rigid binarisms in favour of notions of "mutual imma." Deconstruction also dismantles the hierarchy of "original" and "copy". In a Deridean perspective, the curatic prestige of the original does not run counter to the copy; rather, the prestige of the original is created by the copies, without which the very idea of originality has no*

meaning. The film as 'copy', furthermore, can be the 'original' for subsequent 'film adaptation as 'copy' by analogy is not necessarily inferior to the novel as 'original' The Deridean critique of origins is literally true in relation to adaptation. The "original" always turns out to be partially "copied" from something earlier. The Odyssey goes back to anonymous oral formulaic stories, Don Quixote goes back to chivalric romances, Robinson Crusoe goes back to travel journalism, and so on ad infinnition". (8)

The aforementioned issues raised by Stam are pivotal to the general considerations related to adaptation. The question: who is the original author of a piece of creative work is subject to a number of contributors. What is the impact of wars, migrations, marriages trade, re-settlements to the original tale? Who is right to claim originality and what criteria should be used to ascertain originality to a tribe, clan or group of people or individuals?

In the absence of any written source or archival material, ascertaining originality remains a complex and challenging issue. Our focus is not to dwell much on the original tale narrator but to engage on a process of adaptation of the supposed "original" tale to a new form, visible enough to a wider audience in an era of rapid communication and industrial evolution. Our original tale, collected from one part of the nation, may be considered different in different regions of Cameroon or Africa. But who has the claim of originality? Who can trace where the tale was originally conceived and narrated and where it hastravelledovertime and what changes occurred to it during the period of sojourn?

Today, are we right to rely on an individual narrator we encounter in the village, or the group that make up the audience of the storytelling event? Are we certain that certain innovations of the tale are not made to impress on the listener or collector? And what do we leave the village with after the story telling event? Is it the original or counterfeit? Whatever we leave the village or narrator with, is now in the hands of the target audience to continue in the process of mutation.

Therefore, the end product takes on the form of originality without any authorship, but ascribed to a clan, village, or group of people. When we ascribe a tale to a particular geographical entity, for example, the forest and grass fields, we are indirectly saying that the original narrators originate from one of these regions. If we ascribe it to a village, or clan, for example, 'Oroko tales', or 'Ngemba', or 'Kom', or 'Mundani', we are subjecting the tale to a partial place in time. But it is important to note that tales are not the original property of a select or group of people. Tales do not only have a tribal, regional appeal but a universal appeal, in so far as the message is useful not only to the tribe or clan where it originated, but to a wider community. Though the tales are collected from particular regions, our intention is to adapt the tales so that they address universal needs and aspirations of people living in other parts of the world. Therefore, any tale ushering unity and solidarity to the different peoples and religions of the world is worth adapting in an era of globalization.

Semiotics

According to the *Oxford Concise Dictionary of Literary Terms*, Semiotics or Semiology is:

> *the systematic study of SIGNS, or more precisely, of the production of meanings from sign systems, linguistic or non-linguistic...The Semiotic approach to literary works stresses the production of literary meanings from shared CONVENTIONS and codes; but the scope or written language to other kinds of communicative systems such as cinema, advertising, clothing, gesture and cuisine. (232-233)*

Transforming the oral tale into play, film and comic strips for textbooks and moving images necessitates a mastery of language, movements and sign systems proposed by semioticians. J.A. Cuddon says that Semiotics goes out of language and examines 'human bodily communication' known as "Kinsemics" and "primemics". Cuddon goes on to say that *"in literary criticism semiotics is concerned with the complete signifying system of a text and the codes and conventions we need to understand in order to be able to read it* (853-854).

The language, pictures, illustrations and dialogue of selected tales form part of signifying system codes and conventions necessary in making the narrator and the audience understand and appreciate them within the present context of a global cultural matrix. A cartoon in its textual form and in moving images can teach and entertain students in a classroom situation, a family seated in front of a television screen and the general public that is interested in cartoons. This also applies to a play, a song and a movie.

A Newcastle educational website on Alberti's Window of Fine Art and Theory quotes the words of Jonathan Richardson in *An Essay on the Theory of Painting"* published in 1725 which states:

> *Painting is that pleasant, innocent amusement but it is more; it is of great use as being one of the means whereby we convey our ideas to each other, and which in some respects has the advantage over all the rest. And thus it must be ranked with these, and accordingly esteemed not only as an enjoyment, but as another language.... And this is a language that is universal; men of all nations hear the poet, moralist, historian, divine or whatever other character the painter assumes, speaking to them in their own mother tongue.(1)*

Alberti goes on to mention that in Western society, there has been a great shift from a text-based to a visually dependent culture with images being of prime importance. This impact is on academic theory, which has been dominated by text not picture. According to him recent adherence to the pictorial in academic circles has moved visual representation to a central position and strengthens the debate between the linguistic and the pictorial. Such debate is making its way into the homes and academic centres in parts of Africa through cartoons in children's books and television programmes from Asia, Europe and America. He adds that *"any emphasis on the study of how pictures work in perceptual and cognitive terms must be balanced by a study of the relationship between social/ political power and the power of images"(1).* It is within this context that selected tales of the forest and grass fields of Cameroon are relevant in defining their educational, social, economic, and political importance in a great move towards peace, solidarity, unity and poverty alleviation.

Glory writing on *"Open-Source Movies'* states that *"some people have a story they want to tell, but can't choose their own clothes very well, let alone choose effective costumes for their cast"* (1). She proposes that *"what is needed is a framework in which creative contribution can be swapped in and out independently"* (1). She outlines some aspects of movie production that should be allowed to vary independently. These include the *"overall story, the breaking up of the story into scenes, scene selection and order, overall mood and architectural style, how the characters move around within scenes, character design, costumes and lighting"* (1).

Charles S. Pierce (2006) defines a sign or representation as something which stands to somebody for something in some respect or capacity. He adds that it addresses somebody and creates in the mind of that person an equivalent sign, or a more developed sign. This sign according to Pierre stands for something, its objects in reference to a sort of idea which he sometimes refers to as the ground of the representation.

He identifies three branches of semiotics connected with the ground, the object and the 'interpretant'. The assertion "the first pure grammar", which ascertains what must be true of the representation of every scientific intelligence, is used in order to embody any meaning. The second is logic proper which according to Pierre is the formal science of the conditions of the truth of representations. The third is pure rhetoric which ascertains the laws by which in every scientific intelligence one sign gives birth to another and especially one thought bringing forth another.

Pierce summarizes sign as follows:

> *A sign or Representatamen is a first which stands in such a genuine triadic relation to a second, called its objects as to be capable of determining a Third, called its interpret ant, to assume the same triadic relation to its object in which it stands itself to the same object.* (6)

Pierre points to three Tracheotomies of signs which he describes thus:

> *According to the first division, a sign may be termed a Qualisign a sinsign, or a legisign.*

> *A Qualisign is a quality which is a sign. It cannot actually act as a sign until it is embodied; but the embodiment has nothing to do with its character as a sign.*

> *A sinsign---- is an actual existent thing or event which is a sign. It can only be so through its qualities; so that it involves a qualisign, or rather, several qualisigns. But these qualisigns are of a*

peculiar kind and only form a sign through being actually embodied.

A legisign is a law that is a sign. This law is usually established by men. Every conventional sign is a legisign [but not conversely] it is not a single object, but a general type which, it has been agreed, shall be significant. Every legisign signifies through an instance of its application, which may be termed a Replica of it. Thus, the word "the" will usually occur from fifteen to twenty-five time on page---. Each single instance of it is a Replica. The Replica is sinsign. Thus every legisign requires sinsigns. But these are not ordinary sinsigns, such as are peculiar occurrences that are regarded as significant. More would the Replica be significant if it were not for the law which renders it so (7-8).

The tales under study may be considered as sinsigns when narrated or retold over and over. They may also be considered a replica of the original tale. Once the tale has been adapted by many people and in many communities for special purposes and events, it may be considered a legisign which checks individual and communal actions with the aim of correcting and moralising the audience. In the second tracheotomy, Pierre considers a sign as an Icon, an index or a symbol. He describes them as follows:

An Icon is a sign which refers to the object that it denotes merely by virtue of characters of its own, and which it possesses, just the same, whether any such object actually exist or not. It is true that unless there really is such an object, the Icon does not act as a sign, but this has nothing to do with its character as a sign. Anything whatever, be it quality, existent individual, or law, is an Icon of anything, in so far as it is like that thing and used as a sign of it. (8)

The tortoise, for example, brought in the process of adapting tale No 3 is recognized as an icon of a trickster. This explains why it succeeds in tricking the Leopard to release the monkey and then jumps back into the pit he earlier dreaded.

On the other hand, index, according to Pierce:

is a sign which refers to the object that it denotes by virtue of being really affected by that object. It cannot, therefore be a Qualisign, because qualities are whatever they are independently of anything else. In so far as the index is affected by the object, and it is in respect to these that it refers to the object. (8)

A symbol, he also points out:

is a sign which refers to the object that it denotes by virtue of law, usually an association of general ideas, which operates to cause the symbol to be interpreted as referring to that object. It is thus itself a general type or law that is in a legisign. As such, it acts through a Replica. (8)

In the third tracheotomy, he points out that a sign may be termed a Rheme, a Dicosign or Dicent sign or an Argument defined as follows:

> *"A Rheme is a sign which, for its interpretant, is a sign of qualitative Possibility, that is, is understood as representing such and such a land of possible object. Any Rheme, perhaps will afford some information; but it is not interpreted as doing so"* *(90)*

> *" A Dicent sign is a sign which for its interpret ant, is a sign of actual existence, it cannot therefore be an Icon which affords no ground for an interpretation of it as referring to actual existence. A Dicisign necessarily involves as a part of it, a Rheme, to describe the fact which it is interpreted as indicating". (90)*

> *"An Argument is a sign which for its interpretant, is a sign of law. Argument is a sign which is understood to represent its object in its character as sign.(90)*

Roland Barthes (1968) states that in a normal system whose signs are drawn from a cultural code, what gives the system its originality is that the number of readings of the same lexical unit or lexia varies according to individuals. He adds that the variation in readings is not anarchic but depends on practical, national, cultural, aesthetic knowledge invested in the image. According to Barthes, it is as though the image presented itself to the reading of several different people who can well co-exist in a single individual. It is in this light that the tales under study are examined. They appear as different images to the different people of the forest and grass fields but they are understood by these people in terms of aglobal Cameroonian culture of solidarity, harmony and peaceful co-existence. Therefore, a Cameroonian tale can conveniently travel to any part of the country and be understood because of the cultural awareness of varied cultures that exist. At a practical level, the tales address the different needs of the community where they are created or narrated. At a national level they express the hopes and aspirations of the different peoples of Cameroon. At the cultural level, they point to the different cultural realities of the different voices in the tale.

Applied theatre research according to Aloysius Van Kesteren (1984) is also relevant to this study because it consists of a history as well as a methodology of theatre application" According to Kesteren, theatre research can be used as an auxiliary discipline to other fields, to socio-cultural institutions, persons or groups, or phenomena which are non-scientific in nature. On this note, Kesteren poses the following question: how can theatre research be used as a tool for tackling problems that have didactic, critical pedagogical, sociological, psychological and theatrical implications. This study is part of the process of providing fundamental and necessary methodology that situates theatre and comic strips in the confines of empirical science. Colourful story books which are a by-product of this study can be used in the teaching of English language, literature, health and environmental education, human rights and civic education both at the nursery, primary and secondary schools. The dramatization of the tales can enhance the theatrical process which is destined towards addressing issues such as poverty, poaching, AIDS, unemployment and ignorance in the rural and semi-urban areas under the canopy of theatre for development. Promoting the story telling event in homes provide avenues for relaxation after a hard day's work, thereby fighting stress and other related psychological ailments. Transforming the tales into dramatic forms for dummy shows and popular events like carnivals and festivals enhances the theatrical process in communities where these events are regularly organized.

Theatre semiotics is relevant to the understanding of the process of transforming the oral text into play text. The play text cannot be considered complete without the stage and other technical facilities associated with the stage. Elaine Aston and George Savona (1991) pose a vital question: "why theatre semiotics? In providing an answer to the question, they opted to view theatre semiotics as a methodology, a way of working, approaching theatre in order to open up new practices and possibilities of 'seeing', and not as a theoretical position. It is within this context that we intend in this study to apply new ways of transforming Cameroonian oral narratives into plays for both the stage and the screen.

Aston and Savona (1991) observe that in most academic institutions, drama has, until relatively recently, been taught as a branch of literary studies, as dramatic literature divorced from the theatrical process. It is in this wise that we observed that most playwrights have tended to avoid the oral sources in their plays and instead focused on daily happenings and stories concerning human beings. They fail

to understand that animal tales can be acted using human characters and the outcome will be a fulfilling theatrical experience. In a bid to create meaning, communicated through systems of encodable and decodable signs, they state that in the case of drama, this has involved both the development of new ways of interrogating the text and the generation of a methodology or 'language' with which to tackle the complexity of the theatrical sign-system. They propose documenting and seeing how meaning is generated through the elements involved in the scripting of drama and how meaning is created within a performance context. Such an approach raises the following questions; is the oral text void of meaning as an entity? Is it incomplete when narrated during the story telling event? Is it void of dramatic/theatrical qualities? Can it have more meaning when actually brought on stage in front of a live   ?
Before providing answers to these questions, it is important to adopt an approach which invites us to look at how drama and theatre are created, taking into consideration aspects such as scenery and costumes.

In order to facilitate this process they refer to the Swiss Linguist, Ferdinand de Saussure who advocated a structural study involving both the 'diachronic' (historical) and synchronic (current) dimensions of language. They affirm that what emerged from Saussure's work was an understanding of language as a sign-system in which the linguistic sign was further presented in binary terms as 'signifies' and 'signified' or 'sound-image' and 'concept'. They illustrate all these in the following words:

The two sides of the linguistic sign are arbitrary, which enables language to be a self-regulating, abstract system, capable of transformation. It is through the interplay of similarities and differences between signifiers that meaning is created, and, in order to understand this, a structuralist approach is required in which the 'parts' of, language are considered in relation to the 'whole'. In the light of this, it may be understood that language is the sign-system by which people mediate and organize the world. (6)

According to Georges Mounin (1985), it was the linguist, Ferdinand de Saussure, who extracted the word semiology from its various technical uses in French and introduced it into current scientific language usage. He states that Saussure referred to semiology as a science that studies the life of signs within society and sometimes refers to it as "signology" which is part of social psychology and consequently of general psychology. Mounin points out that Saussure even included "rites", "polite formulas", "customs" and "fashion" as sign systems transmitted through formal social learning, and like natural language, created to ensure communication between subjects belonging to the same community. Mounin also states that Saussure also mentioned writing, the deaf-mutes' alphabet, and military signals as examples of explicit systems of communication.

While answering the question, "What is a sign?" Mounin refers to Pierce, who proposed a tripartite classification of signs in order to clarify the ambiguities created by traditional Greek Usage. These include symbols which correspond to

Saussure's arbitrary signs, index which are indices used by Prieto and other scholars, also referred to as the symptoms of medicine, icons which correspond to Saussure's symbols. Mounin, while elaborating on the notion of sign states:

> *Saussure's contribution was to throw light on the following fact: a sign is composed of a signifier, which is an observable phenomenon (the noise produced by my mouth when I say "house", the drawing that reproduces the outline of a cow on a cream-colored red-rimmed metal triangle, etc). The signifier gives information about another phenomenon, this time non-observable, which is the signified of the sign (which approximately corresponds in my mind and in my language to the concept "cow" or the phrase "cattle crossing. (23)*

Mounin also points to the arbitrariness of a sign system which according to Saussure is an indication that there is no relationship of similarity or necessity between the signifier and the signified. He states for example that there is no relationship of necessity between a white-barred red disk and the idea of access forbidden to all vehicles since one could signify the same thing with a yellow triangle, a green hexagon, or a red triangle. Illustrating a lion, for example, as a character in a comic strip or cartoon may pass for a symbol of power and strength in one community and a symbol of authority and dignity in another. In the grass field region of Cameroon, for instance, the carved lion, in front of a palace represents authority, leadership and dignity usually reserved for the fon and his notables. Because of the dense nature of the forests, the lion ceases to be recognized as a symbol of authority because of the dangers and traps which it cannot perceive around her. The elephant because of its size and strength to pull down trees and shrubs assumes this position of authority. The elephant tusks and carvings in front of the chief's palace are symbols of its authority and dominance.

Transforming the oral tale into plays for the stage revolves around the issue or debate between live and technologically mediated performance raised by Philip Auslander (2008) who states categorically that audiences witness theatre actors in the moment of performance but see performances by film actors only long after the actors have done their work. On this note, he affirms that stage acting is temporally immediate to its audience in a way that film acting is not. He raises the following questions while considering the fate of live performances in the twenty-first century:

> *Is liveness an objective characteristic of performance? Are there necessary or sufficient conditions that, if met, qualify a performance as live? What degree of technologically mediation is permissible before a performance ceases to be live - - -? Or is liveness primarily an effective experience on the part of the audience rather than a characteristic of the performance – are performance live to the extent that we experience them that way as an audience - -? (117)*

The need to move from a story telling event around a fireside, or market square, in a parlour to a stage raises the questions: which is livelier? And which is more technologically mediated? Does this account for the decline in the attendance of stage plays? If yes, what can be done to mediate between live and technologically performances? Should the distance between the stage and the audience be so wide? Should sound and other voice enhancing devices be radically removed? Should the audiences be part of the experiences being enacted by the actors? This takes us to performances which concern and affect the lives of the audience directly in a community. With the active performance of members of that community in bringing the show to live, our consideration takes us to the live dummy shows for kids, community live theatre which are interactive such as carnivals, enactments in cultural festivals, and bonanzas. We are not advocating for the destruction of theatre houses, but for theatre to be brought closer to the audience that live it.

This brings us to the issues raised by Della Pollock (2005, p.120) who examined the narrated event and the narrating event (the telling of it in the present). He raises the views of Richard Bauman (1990) who affirm an inextricability of the 'saying' and the 'said' and who favours performance as the living tissue that connects story and event in tenuous processes of meaning-making and Barbara Myerloff who considers cultural performances such as the enactment of rites, rituals, and ceremonies of normative values and selves as the processes by which normative values and selves are made. Pollock affirms that Bauman and Myerhloff hold that narrative performance which is telling the told as a pivotal practice of cultural crisis.

While examining 'witnessing' within the context of performance, Pollock raises the following questions:

> *What happens when the inter subjection of the listener becomes a performance in its own right? When the listener becomes a witness to what she has heard? In this wise, Pollock states that: "the performance of oral history becomes a critique of defining discourses; a poeisis, of mutual change; a reparative intervention; and a translation of the relationship between the teller and listener into that between multiple listeners arose boundaries of time and place, such that all are induced into performing a new-renewed ethic of imagination and action. (128)*

It is on this note that Pollock affirms:

> *Within the frame of a performative culture, the oral history is itself a itself a repetition without stable origins. It is a form of cultural currency that flows among participants. As such, it does not 'belong' to any one teller. Its vitality lies in exchange, at the dialogical intersection of teller and listener. (128)*

While considering the qualities of competency, intensity, and emergency, Pollock states that Bauman argue for the power of performance to change structures of social relations and stating that many scholars and practitioners have relied on the performance of oral history to achieve social change structures of social relations. He also points out that many scholars and practitioners have relied on the performance of oral history to achieve social change by "breaking silence" amplifying previously unheard voices, and/or entering new stories into the historical record.

New Historicism

New Historicism in the United States of America, according to J.A Cuddon (1991), was heralded by Stephen Greenblatt, Jerome McGann and Marjorie Levinson and in Britain by Marilyn Butler. They constantly question the relationship between history and literature. Robert Con Davis and Ronald Schleifer affirms that according to Stephen Greenblatt, history is divorced from textuality, while Hayden White views history as a narrative sequence marked by inexplicable gaps or ruptures.

Thomas Fish and Jennifer Perkins hold that new historicists argue that *"texts are always intimately connected to their historical and social context, especially perhaps when texts attempt to repress the context"* (1). Seen from a psychoanalytic viewpoint, they intimate that history serves as the repressed unconscious of literature. A study of selected tales from the forests and grass fields of the South West and North West regions conform to the present historical and scientific developments in a global world with growing competition from regional and international groupings apparent and commonplace. The present social context is driving closer to one of individualism and a proliferation of diverse forms of entertainment, communication, dress and speech patterns. One can sit in a room today and access many forms of entertainment through television and via the Internet, which were formerly only available at cultural age-group gatherings during socio-cultural festivals. Today, one can sit in his parlour in Cameroon and take part in a live concert in New York on the television and through the Internet.

New Historicists also reject the western tendency to write history from the top downwards or in grand narrative standpoints. They are more concerned with what Lyotard considers as "petits récits" or "little narratives" and how they participate in the consolidation and maintenance of the status quo. Here, even those considered as less important in the society can also participate in maintaining existing power structures.

The tale, which is being neglected in favour of the novel, television and Internet, accounted, accounts and will continue to account for a moral, peaceful and united social environment. These tales though scattered, neglected and poorly preserved, play the role of conflict resolution where state and international conventions have fail. Though considered as "little narratives", their importance rival legal dictates and minimise force as a recurrent means of conflict resolution and settling disputes. Today, we can affirm that the breakdown of existing moral and socio-political structures may be partly due to the dwindling value of storytelling.

Commenting on textuality, Fish and Perkins (2002) also affirm that new historicists examine texts for their historicity as they would for any historical phenomenon no matter how trivial or less important. According to them, Madonna videos or Renaissance miniature portraiture can be analysed as any literary text. Much attention should therefore be given to tales and other narratives which have been written but are presently being neglected by the educational authorities, policy makers and the reading public. These texts explain and expound on the global historical trends of Africa in relationship with the rest of the world.

Davis and Schleifer (1989) quote Leonard Tennenhouse's words, which allude to the history of a culture as a history of all its products with literature, social organisation and legal apparatus being products of this culture. They go on to mention:

> *Both Marxism and new historicism recognise in literary texts, as Catherine Belsey says "not 'knowledge' but ideology itself in all its inconsistency and partiality." They situate literary criticism in a larger framework of cultural criticism, what Eagleton called "rhetoric' and 'discourse theory'. Such theory above all attempts to understand literature as historically situated practices that encompass power as much as knowledge. (375)*

Transforming culture into feasible realities requires the use of artistic ornaments, which are usually accompanied by design and illustrations that communicate a particular message or worldview to a particular community or a broader world populace. Such an attempt can only be successful if semiotics is integrated into all aspects of cultural studies.

Heda Jason (1977) while assessing the relation between oral literature and society states:

> *It is a commonly held opinion that oral literature is a kind of "reflection" or "native ethnography" of its society. This means that a direct relationship between society and its oral literature is assumed, society being the primary factor in the relationship and oral literature the secondary. If so, it may be possible to get fairly direct information about a society from its oral literature. (277)*

He points out that according to this opinion, which feeds from the Boasian school of thought, "a folktale is "text" which may "reflect a model or typical mental content of the people in a society". He refers to Kalin et al (1966,p.570), who hold that they are data that deal directly with states of mind, whose thematic content is the thought system of society and which are descriptions of the action or reality system, usually described by the natives in their folktales.

He also focuses on Colby, who refers to Roberts and Sutton-smith (1962) who referred to folktales as describing sanctions and prohibited behaviour or various types of useful behaviour and strategies that function as a catharsis, thereby iterating an individual from the immediacy of his own situation. In this same light Jason adds:

> *The same Boasian idea of a direct relationship between oral tale and society is at the basis of the psychoanalytic approach. If the stories are to be psychoanalytic confessions of a whole society, the two, tales and society, have to have a direct*

relationship, that is a subject and his own fantasies which obviously have to be contemporary to each other. Thus, the societies have other tales, just as it had other tales in the past. (278)

The tale under study is a reflection of not only the psychological and emotional states of the minds of people in these societies. Though set amongst the Bakweris, it is directed towards those who are selfish and wicked towards their fellow man and those who disrespect their parents and elders.

The notion of transforming the oral tale to play, film and comic strips is a relatively new endeavour in the literacy landscape of Cameroon. Adaptation, being a concept that requires creativity has been limited to practical applications.

PART FOUR

Factors in Favour of Adapting the Cameroonian Oral Tale to a Play

The focus of this chapter is to provide arguments and viewpoints that support the adaptation process of the oral tales to plays in both informal and formal learning settings. A historical timeline on the adaptation process will reveal the path taken by other adapting artists and the importance of subjecting the oral tale to a similar path. In this wise the views of scholars, custodians of culture, adapting artists, teachers and storytellers will be examined vis-a-vis their respective ideas and contributions. We shall examine moral aspects in favour of redynamisation, pedagogic and didactic relevance, socio-cultural factors, the tale as facilitator of unity, peace and cooperation, eco-critical relevance, economic values, and the therapeutic values.

Before we delve into the reasons why we think the oral tale should be transformed, it will be important to examine the historical process of adapting the oral tale to plays. Transforming and adapting tales to drama dates back to the days of the Greek. Joe Winston quoting Little (1967, p.9) states that in the distant past, the tribal kings used Mythology to support their dynasties, the aristocracy used it to enhance their prestige, the tyrant to reconcile and appease and democracy to express its conflicts. According to Winston, Little stresses the significance of the stories as bearers of shared meanings which were adapted or translated from one epoch to another in order to legitimize the existing power structures. Winston also adds that by the time democracy had been established in Athens, the tale had become a means for exploring the ethical and political values of the *polis.*

Rosenberg affirms that, in the West, the function of the folktale has changed over time. She regrets that the idea that folktales are a child's entertainment is a modern development. She cites Homer who included folktales in *The Iliad* and *The Odyssey*, epics written in the 8th Century B.C. that were designed to entertain and instruct warriors and other adults, as well as children on the cultural values of ancient Greece. She also intimates that the great sacred texts of both the East and the West have treated folktales seriously; including them as moral lessons not leaving out religious leaders who have included them in their sermons for the same purpose. Throughout history, she points out that the telling of folktales has also been a popular form of entertainment among farmers and labourers, merchants, sailors and other travellers, and household servants. In the 14th Century, she cites the example of Giovanni Boccaccio and Geoffrey Chaucer who incorporated folktales into the *Decameron* and *The Canterbury Tales*, respectively. She goes further to state that the literary folktale was born in France in the mid-17th Century with women of the aristocratic class creating them for their own social gatherings and often putting them into written forms before presenting them. She also points out that late in the 17th Century, the French aristocrat Charles Perrault published his versions of folktales for adults in his social circle and in the 18th Century folktales with moral themes began to be considered appropriate material for children. She affirmed that it was until the nineteenth century that they became truly acceptable as children's literature. She also cites the period between 1812 and 1815, in Germany, when Jacob and Wilhelm Grimm published their folktales, which include composites of different oral versions of the same tale as well as tales based on written sources such as Perrault and Hans Christian Andersen's literacy tales which were published in Denmark in 1835. She intimates that in western cultures, folktales have contributed to a national sense of identity and pride, and they were often developed in response to particular political and social needs. She also claims that this is not unusual especially in China, where myths, legends and folktales had been serving these purposes since the Han dynasty that lasted from 202 B.C. to A.D. 220.

Winston also points to examples of tales that were adapted for stage in the Greek Era. He cites the *Oresteia* by Aeschylus, the story of Agamennon's return from the Trojan Wars, his death in the hands of his wife and her lover and the subsequent trial of matricide and revenge that followed. Winston affirms that although no definite or final solution to the conflict could be offered, the drama ends on a note of civil concord, emphasizing the rational power of justice secured within the civil legislative of Athens. He goes ahead to add that the final play of the cycle, *The Euminedes*, uses myth to extol the necessity of this new moral code, that was included within civic law, as different to the pre-democratic and tribalistic code of family vendetta and vengeance, which continued to play a devastating role in the Athenian society.

In answering the question "why did drama become the medium for the integration and revision of myth in classical Athens?", Winston refers to Bruner who affirm that drama is the natural shape of myth because drama reflects the shape of the personality. In this vein, Winston affirms that it is more convincing to take into account the public, political function of drama and its direct link with earlier communal forms of storytelling in what was still in essence, an oral culture. Other issues raised by Winston include the rallying force of storytelling space, used to bring communities together, the role of theatre where stories were heard rather than read, the role of storytelling in verse developed during shared ritual practices, with theatre as a community activity and the performance belonging to the community not leaving out the role of the chorus which acted on behalf of the audience.

Adapting oral narratives to plays is not a new process in the African literary tradition. There have been considerable efforts made in aspects such as translation and writing. Much has not been done as far as adapting for stage and television. It is important to note that oral tales are no longer transmitted solely by way of mouth. They are now major components of print and audio-visuals as observed by Okpewho:

> *African writers have been in the forefront of the continuing efforts to collect and translate texts from their people's oral traditions, and they have*

done this as a way of advertising the greatness of their indigenous cultures. From Francophone Africa we may mention the Malian novelist A. Hampate Ba, who has translated (with Lilyan Kesteloot) some of the heroic tales, or epics, from the Bambara; the Senegalese Birago Diop, who has done the same for Wolof folktales; and the Guinean Djibril T. Niane, who was the first to provide a classic French translation of the famous Mandinka (Mandingo) epic of Sundiata (Sunjata). In Ghana we have had the poets Kofi Awoonor and Adali-Mortty translating pieces of the traditional poetry of their people into sensitive English. In Nigeria the poet-dramatist Clark has given us the epoch-making edition of "The Ozidi Saga", and even the novelist Chinua Achebe has become involved in translating Igbo folktales especially for young readers (Achebe and Iroaganachi 1972). In East Africa Okot p'Bitek of Uganda led the way in the collection and translation of texts of African oral literature; an example is his translation of folktales "Hare and Hornbill" (1978). In South Africa the pioneering work of Thomas Mofolo in presenting the story of Shaka has inspired the poet Mazisi Kunene to publish the texts of greater epic narratives about the war leader in a notable edition, Emperor Shaka the Great *(1979). There are numerous other such efforts across Africa. (18)*

Okpewho goes ahead to present a second group of writers who have been inspired by oral narratives in producing works related to modern life. On this note he states that:

These writers would like to feel that even though their societies have changed drastically from what they were several generations ago and even though they communicate with the world in a language that is not their own, there must be certain fundamental elements in their oral traditions that they can bring into their portraits of contemporary life. In "Weep Not Child", for instance, Ngugi Wa Thiong'o has evoked the image of the ancestor of the Kikuyu race (Mumbi) in his portrait of the struggle of the Kenyan people against foreign oppression. Wole Soyinka, in many of his writings, has used the image of the Yoruba god Ogun as a symbol for the revolutionary spirit needed to combat the social evils that plague both his country, Nigeria, and the black race as a whole. In poetry, both Okot p'Bitek and Kofi Awoonor have borrowed heavily from the techniques of folk expression in writing about present-day situations. (18)

It is important to note that in Africa, Nigeria presents one of the best examples of the process of redynamising the oral tale based on the Yoruba experience. According to Arinze Adejuno (2009), the process of redynamising the oral tale dates back to when oral traditions were recorded by tape recorders, reel-to-reel recorder to capture the audio aspects of performance which were later transcribed and presented as texts for teaching.

He also points out that as far back as 1959 when the Western Nigerian Television and Western Nigerian

Broadcasting Service (WNTV/WNBS) were established, one of the mandates given to the management was the use of indigenous languages on the station. This saw the involvement of Yoruba travelling theatre practitioners like Hubert Ògúndé, Dúró Ládiípò and Kó Lá Ògunmó Lá in the documentation of oral literature using the theatrical tradition as a means of transmitting Yoruba Oral literature and culture through some radio programmes on air. He also pointed out that the 1970s saw the use of cassette recorders promoted by radio stations. He laments that as a result of the limitations of audio cassettes to capture the audio and visual aspects of oral performance, the Yoruba oral literary scholars had to go in search of new media that would be able to capture the real culture of Yorubá as presented in Yoruba oral performance. Some of the challenges include capturing the social cohesion which the song, art and dance generate, the timbre of the instruments used in classifying poems, the language of drums that the drummer sends to the singer-performer and the dancing audience, the personality of the artist and other aspects which include movements of body parts and audience participation.

In order to resolve the challenges posed by audio recordings, Adejuno points out that the introduction of celluloid in the late 1970s marked the start of visual recordings of oral performances and by 1976, the film industry emerged with the production of Ájáni Ógun by OLá Balógun. A distinctive feature of the film, he pointed out, is the transposition of Yoruba oral poetry into the dramatic traditional form. Due to the expensive nature of celluloid, its limited possibilities of reproduction and circulation, and its inability to properly synchronize the audio and visual aspects of performance, the celluloid was replaced by video recordings. He intimates that through the use of home video, the language and culture of the people could be taught in any part of the world.

Presently, documentation of Yoruba oral literature is now being done using the new media like Ipod, digital video disk (DVD), Video compact disc (VCD), flash drive, MPs, mobile phones, camcorder and computer. This gives the audience access to the performance and enhances the mobility of Yoruba oral literature on internet.

In Cameroon, it is important to note that the process has been abandoned to students and researchers whose efforts in collecting, transcribing and analysing the tale reside in academic milieus. It is of recent that writers like Bole Butake, Gilbert Doho, Victor Epie Ngome, George Ngwane and Musing Derrick have embarked on adapting Cameroon and African history and culture into plays, television documentaries and movies respectively.

Storytelling as a Moralising Factor

Storytelling has always been a vehicle for the proliferation of moral values throughout the world. Moral values such as friendship, love, peace, and solidarity have been passed from one generation to another through stories and facilitated by storytellers, narrators and individual members of the audience. The success of most African families including those of their offsprings has been greatly aided by storytelling. Dorothy S. Blair in a foreword to *Tales of Amadou Koumba*, points out that the role of griots in the community was to instruct and entertain through fables that point a clear moral with virtue rewarded and evil punished. She emphasized that most tales deal with traditional beliefs, village life, traditional hospitality, the solving of village problems and explanations of eating and culinary habits, dress, courtesy and greetings which form part of the education of children. In most urban areas today, there is a systematic decline of moral and spiritual values. Disrespect for parents and elders are commonplace. A display of poor dressing and speech patterns is also common.

Many African stories remind us of our duties and responsibilities in a society affected by greed, individualism, disease and poverty. On this note Mr. Joseph Abwambo intimates that in the evenings, parents used storytelling to educate and moralise their children. He intimated that The *Story of the Tortoise and the Dog* was used to educate young people on the need to be steadfast when embarked on an important mission. In this wise they are advised against any form of distraction until their objectives are attained. He also employed the story of *Tortoise and Hipopotemus* to educate people on the presence of vicious people who fan problems between two persons, and then stand by and watch as they devour each other without the least knowledge of the causes or origin of the crisis. From *The story of John and Mary* narrated by Gobu Daniel the audience learnt that if someone does something bad, his crime will one day be exposed.

Rosenberg points to the touch of great stories on our spirits and the appeal they make for more understanding in handling issues related to human growth and advancement. In this light, the attitudes and behaviour of the characters in the tales remind us of our shortcomings and successes. The moral lessons in these stories enable us to fight some of the social ills of society. The stories also compel us to consider who we are, where we come from and where we are going. In answering these questions, we ponder whether or not we are taking the right decisions. And as we ponder, they instil in children, youth and adults a spirit of respect, cooperation and understanding between the younger and older generation; love between parents and children and between citizens and state institutions. J. Olowo Ojoade points to an array of themes seen through oral literature. These include humility, gratitude, speech and silence, gossip and rumour, co-operation, hospitality, truthfulness and honesty, hypocrisy, taking advice, self and others.

Winston Joe (1998) affirms that children who take active part in dramatic activities are able to learn how to cooperate, own a social identity, be responsible towards one another, understand the importance of rules and self-discipline and also to grow in self-esteem. According to him within a "dialogical" relationship between drama and traditional stories, children will be able to interpret, negotiate and understand moral meanings.

Winston goes further to refer to Lawrence Kohlberg, a foremost theorist and researcher who applied cognitive developmental theories of learning to moral growth, who claims that at heart, morality stands for a set of rational principles of judgement and decisions important for every culture and which include the principles of welfare and justice.

Kolberg's focus, according to Winston, is on an individual's increasing ability to reflect autonomously and selflessly upon the moral principles which can be applied to specific moral dilemmas or problems. The narrative through storytelling therefore plays a vital role in the moral transformation of young children. It is in this vein that Winston intimates that narrative can pass across the "messiness" of reality and the moral life and also something of its thickness and complexity.

Stories widen the horizons of the teller and the listeners, reveal different options to seeing the world and human beings and foster a spirit of community and gainful human interaction. But these virtues are yet to be felt because in many African communities, the writing of stories, especially the folktale seems to have been left in the hands of people who lived in distant parts. May be animal tales are no longer part of our vocabulary because of systematic poaching, chasing and killing of animals from the nearby forests. So their lives are no reference to the social realities of human beings in this modern and fast technological epoch. Tales on recent concerns such as terrorism, crime, environmental degradation, abuse of human rights and pornography, amongst others are not part of tales of human interest.

Winston on this note states that our ability to author the moral self is therefore based on our understanding of the virtues implanted in the social roles we are born into and these are learned in part from the stories which are part of our heritage. It is on this base that this researcher questions the reservoir of our intangible cultural heritage, which is yet to address the plethora of our cultural realities. The question, therefore is what should we do to replenish our intangible cultural basket in the face of a more aggressive Western culture whose stories have been transported to Africa using the most recent and sophisticated technologies powered by electricity, the solar system, space technologies and the internet. Western stories now find safe havens in comic strips, computer games and mobile phones. But the question remains: What moral values are these tales transmitting. From popular tales such as *Lucky Luke* to *Tom and Jerry*, the message is clear– violence, survival of the fittest and the strong and witty gets it all. Yes, this may be a true reflection of the world but should we stand by and watch the world consumed by vice? This research, based on tales with relevant moral attributes, will reveal how their transformation into plays will go a long way to expose a counter value system based on the respect of human values such as peace, harmony, respect and social cohesion.

According to Richard Moorse (2009), our ancestors obviously understood the dangers produced through a loss of connection. Moorse states that when we consider the widespread alienation faced by today's young people especially young people from their parents, young people from teachers, and young from the young, we can further appreciate their wisdom. On this note, Moorse sees the need for inclusion and bonds of connection. He cites a host of violent attacks perpetrated by youths who do not feel loved and who do not have a sense of belonging. He sees theatre providing a panacea to these young people struggling to feel loved and appreciated in a society guided by individualism, selfishness and greed.

As we examine or ponder over these moral aspects, one tends to discover a reversal of roles and attitudes in the past and present society. Young people today have lost touch with these moral values and are openly seen challenging their parents, elders and other elderly persons in their society. Moral standards in most schools today are falling because of the absence of storytelling in the curriculum. Little or no attention is given to storytelling. In an interview with Chief Mesumbe Anthony Nkumbe of Muantah-Muambong, he laments that children do not have respect for elders today. He intimated that parents cannot influence the choices young people make. He blames parents, whom he says, should have the moral obligation to bring up their children. He proposes that parents should find time once a week to sit down and tell stories and hold other discussions. Dr. Eben Njang Simon, an educationist and former Secretary of the Cameroon Baptist Convention (CBC) Education Board, blames parents who join their children in watching television programmes and minimising the telling of stories. On a sentimental note, he said that some of the television items make him unhappy and those who were brought up in Christian morality actually shed tears. He recounts his experience while he was in Britain, stating that all the films having pornographic undertones were shown between the hours of 12 midnight and 4 a.m. in the morning. He decried violent films shown over the television and laments that they have influenced terrorist activities today. He proposes educative and development- oriented films. He recounts an experience in Britain in 1973 wherein a film was shown over the British Broadcasting Corporation (BBC) depicting an armed robbery in a bank.

The following day, the same methods used in the film were used in robbing a bank in London. He said that to some of them, it was a cultural shock. He suggests participation in international cultural festivals and the use of cartoons as a means of projecting the Cameroon culture to other parts of Africa and the rest of the world. Of a total of 121 questionnaires filled by respondents between the ages of 9-31 and above, 73 chose the option that the morale or lessons learnt are what attracts their interest in the prose narratives. This is a signal to the importance of promoting morality in any given community.

Frantz Fanon's comments on national culture centre on the fact that every time the storyteller relates a fresh episode to his public, he presides over a real invocation and the existence of a new type of man is revealed to the public. The experience, according to him, can take up highway robbers and remodel them. There is therefore need today to redynamise storytelling and define the roles of the narrator, the script and the audience. These three, when managed, can help to improve upon the falling morals of the society crippled by selfishness, greed, tribalism and lies telling.

The Oral Tale as an Educative and Pedagogic Tool

Apart from moralising, oral tale and the storytelling process remain vital tools in transmitting, preserving and consolidating educational values and concepts. The importance of education in the social, economic, psychological and mental growth of any individual remain the concern of individuals, groups, societies and nations all over the world. Abandoning storytelling is like allowing a vital part of one's body to perish. The impact on the rest of the body will, no doubt, lead to the destruction of the whole body. This section will reveal aspects, views and notions that support the redynamisation of the storytelling event in an era of globalisation. Patrick Mbunwe Samba (1985) complained that very little is being done in formal education to exploit the rich oral literature to serve educational ends. Efforts in the past to introduce oral tradition, he wrote, had been sporadic, uncoordinated and inconsistent. This has continued till date, as there is no clear distinction between oral literature and the bulk of western educational material. As a remedy, he states:

> *The influence and adoption of a western literary culture on our traditional oral literature should be made to help rather than hinder us. As a matter of fact, oral literature should become an all-important subject in all our educational institutions at all levels in all countries of Africa. (91)*

He goes on to decry the conception that storytelling is a subject fit only for nursery and junior primary classes. He states that this is "an oversimplification of an otherwise complex subject", for universities in the developed world give courses in storytelling. He concludes by affirming that he has tried to show that storytelling is an important part of oral literature and that there can be a systematic structured course on it for all levels of the school system that will certainly improve their communicative competence, their reading and listening skills and the acquisition of vocabulary and other language structures.

Storytelling plays an important role through special occasions, events and among families, groups and especially during the teaching and learning processes. It is a major component of human experiences, communities and cultures. Since stories are transmitted orally, the story telling event provides an avenue for lively didactic process. Storytelling is therefore one of the techniques and methodologies used by teachers in the teaching and learning process. A host of subjects can be effectively taught using storytelling. The tales selected are didactic in nature and therefore useful teaching aids and tools. Stories have the tendency to hold the learner's attention and engage his or her imagination. Children love listening to stories especially stories narrated to them by their parents, grandparents and teachers. In rural areas, children love listening to tales in their mother tongue, especially when they are spiced by riddles and jokes. It is usually an opportunity for children to sit in the company of their parents and learn new words and expressions in their mother tongue. They are comfortable listening and understanding than reading. They get bored reading a tale than listening to that same version either narrated by their parents and teachers. They are also excited when it comes to question-and-answer session, especially when there are elements of motivation. Some of the things that keep them alive and awake are the gestures, mime and pictures used by the storyteller to illustrate what he is narrating.

Storytelling is a useful methodology in the modern language classroom that employs the communicative approach to teaching. The narrators are not only exposed to the languages usage but to the cultural aspects of the area where the tale is narrated. A host of the tales from the grass fields and the forest are not only imbedded with linguistic patterns but with an array of socio-cultural knowledge of the cultures of the grass fields and forest of Cameroon.

The tales being transformed either as film or play scripts make repetitive use of vocabulary and structures that enable the child to master certain words and phrases. It is important to note that during the storytelling event, the four language skills of reading, speaking, writing and listening come in play. In this wise, the teacher makes available the translated version of the tales and allocate some time for them to be read. After the reading exercise he may ask selected pupils to recite what they have read or pose a host of questions that elicit different responses to different issues. The students may be posed with some didactic questions that necessitate them to provide the answers through writing. And the teacher may decide to read out a story to test their listening skills. A storytelling event can therefore provide a forum for the effective application of the four language skills.

The storytelling event is a forum to motivate and stimulate the imaginations of children and to get them involved in the storytelling process. In this wise they are able to think about the experiences of the different characters in the tale, and to relate these events to their lives and experiences. These therefore enable them to see life from different stand points and to imagine what it feels like to be someone else. While it provides them with an opportunity to think and broaden their horizons, it enables them to have an opportunity to learn different aspects such as human rights, conflict resolution, peace, unity and solidarity.

Storytelling lso enable the pupils to broaden their social skills while learning to interact with others thereby building friendship, love and solidarity. It also enhances the learner's literary competence and his or her ability to study, understand and enjoy literature. Different aspects such as plot, character, themes, dialogue, and imagery are acquired from the tales. The learner is also able to improve on his pronunciation, and interaction based on the models provided by the storyteller, who is usually the teacher of English. Storytelling also facilitate communication between the storyteller and his/her audience, especially when both take part in narrating the tale, providing feedback, predictions and evaluating the moral lessons and social standpoints.

In order for storytelling to be effective as a pedagogic tool, the performance element should be emphasized by the teacher. In this wise, the teacher must dramatise the story to render it engaging and interesting. In order to dramatise the action, the students should be assigned to play the roles of the different characters. It is also advised that the teacher also should take part in the action as an actor. In essence his role will guide the students in order to vary the pitch, volume and tempo of voice, make effective use of mime and gestures, maintain eye contact with the learners, make good use of acting space, employs different voices for different characters.

Henry A. Giroux (1993) states that Claire Doyle demonstrates a keen sense of the importance of drama as a pedagogical practice that binds theory and practice on the one hand, and the politics of representation and the body on the other. Giroux adds that Doyle uses drama as a form of cultural production to enable students to use their bodies and minds in the process of being able to link language and experience, desire and affirmation, and knowledge and social responsibility. He also points out that Doyle's approach engages students in actual plays as part of a broader attempt to understand themselves and their relationship with others and also to learn how the dynamics of power operate in the intersection of school and society. He goes further to intimate that Doyle does not rely on pedagogy of deconstruction, but interested in seeing students write plays as part of a larger pedagogical process of bringing to light their sense of agency and their complex connections with daily life.

Doyle, in his preface, states that:

> *My strongest recollections about teaching in high school are found in the remembered voices of students who used drama to tell their stories. I was often amazed at the stories that were presented, in dramatic form, as if they were fiction. The enactments covered the gamut of stories about friends, mishaps, adventures, loves, and families, of loneliness, fun, horror, and*

happiness. Sometimes the stories left me frozen in my adjudicator's seat because I knew they were not fiction. They were acting out of some joy or some horror that was private to the student. The student found in the drama a place to speak the truth and yet be safe. I learned a lot from those young people and their stories. I am also learning from my graduate students how drama can aid us in our struggle to make sense of the total process of curriculum development (XV-XVI).

According to Doyle, Drama weaves its forceful way through the domains represented by school culture, popular culture, and class culture. Doyle adds that Drama can help break down some of the actual barriers to transformation teaching and learning by exploring new ways of 'going about' the process of schooling. One of these ways, according to Doyle, includes aiding students discover their voices and encouraging teachers to 'trade' in voices of domination for voices of encouragement and empowerment. On this note, Doyle intimates that in many circumstances this requires listening to ourselves and examining what is behind our words rather than shifting language.

Doyle again intimates that there is no real harm in drama as entertainment as long as its other potential is appreciated and used. Drama can be useful to society and in this way serves as a powerful educational tool. Because drama employs words, sound, and images, it can navigate social terrains with a certain degree of ease. He also states that drama, with these words, sounds and images can point, gesture, complain, and promise. He also adds that drama can let the right hand know what the left hand is doing and can also cut away our rituals and institutions and expose memories and promises.

According to Doyle, educators perceive drama as mainly interested in human development and theatre pre-occupied with the acquisition of performance skills. He adds that drama deals with process and theatre with product. Doyle refers to Gavin Bolton, who argues that teachers should think about drama and theatre being at opposite ends of a continuum rather than considered as separate entities. So, Doyle points out those teachers need to be able to move back and forth across the continuum to address the individual needs of their students. In this vein he affirms that critical drama pedagogy concerns itself with the crucial skills of interpreting, questioning, examining, focusing, reflecting, and sharing. Malcolm Ross (1982) realizes that drama, as used in education, must draw from theatre. It is important for educators to value the relationship between experiencing and presenting. This done in a reflective fashion offers real hope for critical pedagogy. Doyle further states:

> *Drama in schools must work to provoke a critical response from its audience and a reflective commitment from its directors and actors. The world of the student must come face to face with the reality of the audience. Here we can see how drama and theatre, as they are traditionally separated, could complement each other. Drama taps the student resources that could be the basis for a script, and theatre presents the developed*

> *play. By building on student resources, teachers can also reinterpret scripted plays. (46)*

The prose narratives have been and continue to serve as useful pedagogic tools in formal and informal learning situations. In basic primary level, the prose narratives remain attractive to children especially the fast rate with which the action is presented, the suspense created by the narrator, the message(s) he passes across which centre on existence of good and evil, and the rewards reserved for the good persons and punishment meted on the wicked and evil ones.

Children are also quick at identifying themselves with the heroes of these tales, especially when their actions and exploits bring in good tiding in the community. The teacher, who plays the role of an educated narrator and harbinger of knowledge is considered as a hero and role model. His or her version of the tale is always true and correct and any attempt by the parents at home to provide them with another version is futile. So, it becomes incumbent for the classroom teacher to learn and master the correct version of the tales in order not to be considered as an under teacher by the parents and other members of the community.

The tale is also a vital weapon in the hands of the teacher. He can use it to transmit a myriad of messages ranging from love, peace, unity, solidarity, discipline, respect for elders, patriotism, harmony, for honour, divine wisdom, to human rights, democracy and the prevention of HIV/AIDS. These are values which the modern narrator can incorporate in the process of transforming the tale into play scripts and comic strips. As a tool in the hands of the teacher, the tale serves as dual purpose; as teaching aid and as useful documentaries of cultural history and tradition.

Mbangwana (1983), states that there is still much to be done with the content of our teaching aids, especially in the primary school. Here aspects of our oral tradition like songs, drawings, proverbs, riddles and tales are absent. He says that our cultural heritage has much in store for educationists. He earlier mentioned that storytelling provides a very efficient medium for entertainment and education in the face of a powerful competition by western and modern forms. He states that despite the impact that the modern media like the radio, cinema and television have over us, storytelling that incorporates all the elements of these media remains the most vital medium of entertainment and education.

Dr. Eben Njang Simon, educationist and Former Secretary of the Cameroon Baptist Education Board (C.B.C.) recalled that many years ago, when he was a teacher, storytelling had an important place in junior classes of the primary schools. The stories, just like the ones narrated by his mother, had profound moral lessons. In a classroom situation, some students were asked to narrate the tales while others had to dramatise or mimic certain aspects of the tale. But today, he has observed that, teachers and educational authorities do not place much importance on this educational and moral aspect of education. Today, storytelling is absent from the school curriculum. Stories that appear in readers and other story books are mere prose passages that are read and analysed in class without any emphasis on dramatisation and the use of songs to build a lively and more participatory atmosphere. Ejedepang Kogge insists that the present curriculum should include storytelling. He feels it will enable students learn more about their culture and also imbibe moral lessons. The stories when narrated will help improve upon their speech and language skills in general. He points out that one difficulty today in the urban areas is overcrowded classrooms. He cites a class of one hundred and twenty pupils and says this number does not help in developing the potential of individual students. Storytelling therefore becomes difficult in such an environment as only a few students actually take part. He proposes that textbook writers for young children should make use of illustrations, pictures and drawings to hold, maintain and sustain the attention of these young readers who usually do not have the patience to read a lengthy prose passage. He finally recalled that all the books he used in the primary school had illustrations. As a remedy, he proposes that the tales should be collected, assembled, codified and transformed into theatrical and motion pieces. He warned that if this is not done, then Western, Arab and American stories will take precedence thereby leading to the loss of our cultural base.

A close look at the university curriculum in Cameroon, for example, displays a wide gap in the study of oral traditions. Studies in traditional languages are also absent. Research in cultural artefacts and their significance including storytelling still leaves much to be desired. In this vein, François Tavenas propose:

> *La principale préoccupation de la communauté universitaire → internationale → devrait → être*

> → *de combattre l'élargissement du "Knowledge gap" entre les nations développés et les pays en émergence, d'éviter que se crée ce que Tebeho Moja (chapitre II) a appelé un "global apartheid"*

> *The main preoccupation of the University community should be to close the knowledge gap between developed and developing countries to avoid what Tebeho Moja calls "global apartheid". (251-252)*

The absence of an in-depth study of African oral traditions in the universities of Africa has created a "Knowledge gap" which is the result of the differences that exists between those in the urban areas and those in the villages. Faced with the proliferation of Western oral forms through the radio, television and internet, "global apartheid" has set in which is working against Africans in favour of the Americans and Europeans. The study aids and programmes in most schools and colleges are pro-west. This has led to a blind admiration by African students of all that is western and a disregard for all that is African and locally bound.

The late chief Bebe II of Banga Bakundu observed that in the days of his youth, a child was considered bright if he could narrate a story. He acknowledged the important role proverbs have played in his life. He intimated that they made him intelligent. He suggested, in an authoritative note, that teachers should include storytelling in their programmes with each student or pupil assigned to tell a story. He went ahead to intimate that school authorities should force students to go home and ask their parents to tell them a story. This will sound impossible in cities, towns and urban villages where most middle-aged parents today cannot even remember, let alone narrate a tale to their children. Transforming the tale into moving images may be a starting point in the discussions centred on the tales.

In answering the question "why should traditional stories lend themselves so readily to moral exploration through drama?" Joe Winston (1998, p.2) intimates:

> *My experience as a teacher and as a head in primary and middle schools was that stories were, indeed, associated with moral education but usually in assembles, where tales from such volumes as Bailey (1981) carried a straight forward didactic message designed to illustrate that, for example, lying could be dangerous, that humility was a virtue and that flatterers should not be trusted. (2)*

In situating the place of drama in the moral process, Winston states that it is commonly accepted in schools and among teachers of drama, that drama plays a vital role in the personal, social and moral education of children. This researcher supports the views of those who not only see drama in the aforementioned light, but attribute the moral decadence in society to the gross neglect of drama as a didactic and moralizing tool. Winston, goes ahead to point to the relationship between drama and traditional stories and their important contribution, when combine, to the moral education of young children. This study, therefore lends itself, to an examination of how selected tales, if dramatised can facilitate the moral renaissance of children and youths trapped in a culture of violence, indecency, corruption and the abuse of basic human rights. On this note, Winston while proposing a historical relationship between drama and myth affirms that drama interrogates, revises and renews the moral values within the myth.

The Oral Tale as Cultural and Identity Marker

As cultural and identity markers, the oral tale reflects the rich cultural values of the society of the learners. While the learners are quick to identify themselves with some of the cultural values related to their socio-cultural backgrounds, they are also able to learn more about their language, history and tradition. The oral tale either in oral or print format is a valuable resource to young people, especially when they are associated with drawings, pictures and other symbols. These pictures which are visual images create a whole array of mental images which remind the learners about the values, wisdom and potentials of their society and some of the individuals who incarnate certain virtues there in.

Can a restoration of Cameroon's culture through storytelling and folklore help in the moral upbringing of youths? In response to this question, we can affirm that transforming the tales into plays, through a process of adaptation, not only create another forum of interaction but transfers the setting of the oral tale from the fireside, to the classroom and other public places. It also shifts the debate from a traditional audience to a modern audience.

The tales form a greater part of reading material relevant in the education of children and youths in Cameroon and Africa in general. The stories that form the foundation of the dialogue in plays, especially tales familiar to children and youth not only attract them to watch the play but incite them to play relevant roles. This is an attempt to bring the children closer to their cultural realities amidst Western and foreign literary material replete in our school milieu. It is important to note that complaints about falling academic standards can be traced to a porous cultural knowledge which they are supposed to learn before being exposed to more Western and alien concepts. The tales, that form the core values of Cameroonian and African literacy traditions, are therefore relevant in laying a strong foundation for the education of children and youths. Revisiting our cultural heritage and foundation as veritable sources of raw material to produce plays will not only revive our culture but serve in bridging the gap created by an imperialist form of education characterized by values alien to the teachings of our ancestors and griots. Mastery, therefore, of the elements that comprise our folklore and tradition is sine qua non to understanding African cultural values, with education being primordial. In Cameroon, the youths and even a greater number of adults have lost touch with the rich folklore and traditions of their different ethnic groups. Many youths, especially those who live in urban areas neither speak nor understand their mother tongues. English language, French and pidgin are used regularly, depending on the social background of the speaker. Since these aspects of the folklore are originally transmitted through mother tongues, those who do not understand their language cannot appreciate their folklore and oral traditions.

The Storytelling event, usually characterized by proverbs, the folktale, songs, puzzles and jokes, make up the rich cultural baskets of most African traditions. In Cameroon, storytelling is usually associated to local and village settings. Those in urban and 'civilized' settings especially in towns and cities have completely lost touch with the practice–the storytelling event – that was the basis of family harmony, learning, the transmission of rich cultural norms and values, ethics and the preservation of culture for future generations. Presently, the situation is made worse with the plethora of communication and technological facilities that have severed the cord that held most families together. While Western movies, soaps and documentaries serve to spread Western cultural values and practices, the African is busy consuming them on the other side. In Africa, the Nigerians, South Africans, Ghanaians, are using their film industries to sell their culture and traditions to other parts of Africa and the rest of the world. Unfortunately, focus is on human interest stories, political, economic and social events.

The folklore has been relegated to the background. In schools and colleges, the situation is made worse because stories that make up our readers and other textbooks are drawn from Western countries and backgrounds. While heroes like Serena Williams, Michael Jackson, Martin Luther King, Malcolm X, James Bond, Charlie Chaplin etc. constitute the characters of stories in the readers, the likes of Martin Paul Samba, Patrice Lumumba, Um Nyobe, Murtala

Mohammed, Nkrumah, Leopold Sedar Senghor, Muammar Khadaffi, Sultan Njoya, and Charles Atangana are yet to find place in story books that dominate our school curriculum. In the same vein our popular animal stories and trickster tales that fascinated children and youths before the advent of television are no longer part of evening conversation. It was during such moments, that the storyteller, usually parents, grandmother, aunt or uncle, or elderly person in the family, employed proverbs, riddles and jokes and songs to hold the audience spellbound and to elicit positive feedback and contribution. It is usually a veritable moment of family communion and re-union. It is also a moment of stock taking, evaluation of individual progress records, settling of family squabbles, disputes and arguments. In essence, it is a veritable moment for the strengthening of family bonds and ties, not leaving out sharing and praises where they are due.

In order to reinstate the lost cultural values, some African writers have embarked on incorporating their folklore in their literary works. Chinua Achebe, popularly known as the father of proverbs, has made extensive use of Ibo proverbs in his works. He is also well acknowledged to have said that "proverbs are the palm-oil with which words are eaten". Achebe's *Things Fall Apart* is considered very successful as a result of the role proverbs play in weaving the story. Generally, proverbs have been used to transmit different aspects of African culture, spread the values of morality, and enforce different aspects of peace and harmony. Amos Tuotuola's *Palm Wine Drinkard*, and Bole Butake's *And Palm-wine Will Flow*, also employ proverbs, relevant in unravelling the plot and explaining different aspects of the culture.

In spite of efforts by writers to preserve Africa folklore in print and written form, many children, youths and adults do not have access to the books. It is not uncommon to find out that in rural areas of Cameroon, many children do not have text books let alone story books and novels. Many parents, when confronted, blame their inability to purchase text books for their children, to poverty and economic crisis. If we go by their arguments, then we can say that the use of story books has failed to transmit our folklore like storytelling did in the past. But the question remains: can storytelling be revived in homes where the television and internet seems to be the most used modes of communication and entertainment?

Can the teaching and performance of folklore at home and in the classroom help in inculcating the lost traditional values formerly transmitted by the oral tale through the storytelling event? The teaching and performance of folklore remain vital educational material and facilitate inter-personal communication between children and their parents and between the teacher and his or her pupils. The folktale which is the focus of this study will be explored as a veritable means of transmitting, preserving and valorisation of the cultures and traditions of not only the forest and grass field regions of Cameroon, but Cameroon and Africa in general.

Robert J. Landy (1982) affirms that tribal people all over the world use dramatic dance to promote the mental health of the community, and the ancient Athenians used it for both education and therapy. Landy also points out that rhetoric was at the heart of medieval learning and intimates that in the Renaissance the speaking of Latin dialogue and the staging of plays were components of the school curriculum. Mme de Maintenon, wife of Louis XIV, established the convent of Saint-Cy, where the girls improvised dialogue and conversation and performed plays by Racine and Corneille. By the nineteenth century, however, drama in schools had dwindled to the production of the occasional school play.

Elements of the oral tradition such as riddles, proverbs and stories reveal the virtues, norms and practices of our ancestors, parents and elders. These virtues when handed down to the young generation will safeguard aspects of history, customs, religion and tradition in a particular society. Greenblatt, in Leonard Tennenhouse's words, affirms this when he states that *"the history of a culture is a history of all its products, literature being just one such product, social organisation another, the legal apparatus yet another, and so on"* (374). Education seems the most vital medium of passing all these values at once. Storytelling as an arm of education ensures this by way of mouth either in a formal or non-formal atmosphere. Redynamising storytelling with the introduction of recent communication and entertainment devices will ease this process in today's world.

Binam Bikoi during the colloquium on the cultural identity of Cameroon in May, 1985 intimated:

> *It could have been expected that the school, having taken the city by storm, would offer the study of our nation's literature among the thousand other subjects offered within its austere framework. On the contrary, it has been systematically excluded under various pretexts. You think I exaggerate? Are there not numerous researchers who devote themselves to collecting and studying oral traditions, including literary traditions? Joking aside... for if a few researchers do transcribe and translate a few works, who can boast with certainty that they will be read? (93)*

Tala also observes that a problem faced in the study of orature on the African continent is that the educational syllabuses on literature do not emphasize orature. In an interview with Kelvin Ngong, he observes that there is an absence of a reading culture in Cameroon. On this note he suggests that Oral literature should be taught in secondary schools because students only learn of the concept for the first time in the university. He suggests that the bare tales be reinforced with pictures so that a mental picture can be created in their minds. He encourages those who do research in oral literature to bring films and photographs of live performances. He also said that students in secondary schools should be made to understand that oral literature is as important as its written counterpart. In primary schools, the pupils should be told the relevance of oral prose narratives like myths and legends to their societies.

Okpewho observes that a larger proportion of the population in Africa today is illiterate or preliterate; but those who seek literate education are growing in numbers. He also affirms that if literacy is going to play a primordial role in the cultural future of African society, then elements of the oral culture should be recovered and fitted into the culture of the written or printed word. The tales under study are parts of the elements of Cameroon oral tradition, which will serve the educational needs of schools and Universities. In a note of finality, Okpewho states that:

> *While there are numerous elements of the oral tradition available for use by our modern writers, we should perhaps recognise that literacy is here to stay and has a discrete character of its own; the best justification for the tradition is not a whole sale transfer into literate art but a judicious selectiveness which will prove its adaptability to changing circumstances. While I applaud the recourse to tradition, I really do not see the point in some of our writers carrying on as if orality is our destiny. (23)*

These proposals aimed at giving new impetus to the tales will match with the present expectations of youths, elders and politicians who live in urban areas so that they are not considered lost and out of touch with what obtain in the villages and rural areas. Adaptability of aspects of oral tradition therefore bridges the gap between the literate and illiterate, the rural masses Jond city dwellers and the culturally profane and urban mundane populace. It will also kill the spirit of mistrust that exists when these two groups of people meet.

According to Winston:

> *Many teachers understand, for example, the conflicts that can exist between the family and the professional community and the difficulties involved in attempting to be a good parent and a good professional at one and the same time. The school is the forum where different communities of interest meet and one of its fundamental challenges is to forge itself into an institution conscious of its role as a community where certain agreed virtues are cultivated and learned. In fact, in an era when communities of family, work and place are increasingly unstable, the school remains one of the fixed, communal spaces where this cultivation can be trusted to take place (175).*

He adds that *"in fact, schools must of necessity define and promote particular virtues such as industry, responsibility, honesty and respect for others and draw up either implicit or explicit rule systems to encourage conformity to them"*(175). In Cameroon and other African countries south of the Sahara, they are far from realizing these ideals. Faced with inappropriate curriculum, lack of staff, research facilities, low income for teachers, lack of space, and didactic material, an unhealthy student-teacher relationship, the school is yet to be an epitome of moral consciousness and development. In an atmosphere of poverty and unemployment, school dropouts form a menace to the global environment. Unfortunately, the teaching of theatre and drama is absent from the primary school curriculum, while in the secondary schools, students encounter a drama text from mid-secondary levels in the literature class. Theatre or drama is not taught as a distinct subject on its own right. So, drama, being one of the weapons of social and moral change is absent as a subject in the school curriculum. The choice of schools therefore is an attempt in penetrating a wild field with untamed animals. The process, therefore of using drama to inculcate moral values in the school milieu is daunting and requires collaboration both from the administration, the staff, students and parents. Doyle affirms that drama has had a long and ambiguous history in education and schools have traditionally upheld the importance of drama and the arts in education.

The Oral Tale as a Cultural Database

Storytelling remains a vital tool for the collection, preservation, and transmission of cultural values, norms and practices. Ejedepang Koge in an editorial on the culture of the Bakossi people holds that if culture is static, society will make no progress. It must be dynamic in incorporating new and useful elements borrowed from other cultures or internally evolved. This section will raise the following questions. Is there a Cameroonian culture? Is it static or dynamic? Does it embrace new and foreign forms? Are these forms playing a pivotal role in determining the lifestyles, attitudes and worldview of Cameroonians? Are there avenues available to check excesses and to sustain lasting values? Is storytelling exposed to the marauding and invading western and individualised culture? Are there ways to incorporate these foreign forms but still retains the Africanness in the rendition of African oral narratives? Views of scholars, critics, men of culture and researchers will say if transforming and redynamising aspects of oral tradition to fit into new and modern forms will help in preserving the cultural values of Cameroon.

The problem of a Cameroonian cultural identity was diagnosed by a group of researchers and critics and solutions proposed during a colloquium from 14 May to 19 May 1985 in Yaoundé organised around the theme: "The Cameroonian cultural identity through its literary and artistic forms of expression" under the auspices of the Minister of Culture, Francois Sengat Kuo. A similar exercise took place earlier from January 28th to February 1st 1985 in the University of Yaounde under the cover "Colloque International sur la literature Orale de l'Afrique Contemporarine: Approaches Théoriques et Pratiques" under the auspices of the Chancellor of Yaoundé University, Professor Joseph Owona. In the colloquium of May 1985, Dr. Pie-Claude Ngumu (1985) in a general introduction to "theme and methodology" laments:

> *The Cameroonian is something, which he is not aware of. He is unaware of it precisely because he is captive to the torment caused by the shock of yesterday's ancestral values and today's foreign ones. It is in this cultural storm that the Cameroonian moves and struggles to give himself an identity and to construct a world where he feels secure and in agreement with himself. Does his struggle have any chance of success? (20)*

In an attempt to answer this question, the idea of redynamisation and building a cultural bridge was born as a solution to secure and locate this lost Cameroonian. This will entail harmonising aspects of his past and present with foreign values to create a tri-symbiosis or trinity that secures his identity as a Cameroonian, an African and a world personality. This will not entail the creation of a new individual but the shaping of one who is open and prepared to accept other cultural values but at the same time preserving his ancestral and national identities. Binam Bikoi on a serious note affirms:

> *However, I think it useful to say that nothing in Cameroon is more threatened today than our national traditional literature. Not far from the year 2000, under the double fact of former colonial domination and the absence of a more committed cultural policy to defend and illustrate positive inherited values, the oral literature in our country is receding fast. Created as it was to be delivered to a listening public, it is obliged to accept whatever audience it can find nowadays-the village square in the moonlight having been deserted in favour of the bar under neon lights of the town. (93)*

He goes ahead to quote works like "Akoma Mba", "Hitong's Sons", "Kéki la Njambé" which are now like Afo-Akom, housed in a museum as museum pieces. Close to twenty years later, the words of Binam Bikoi still remind us of our laxity in handling issues of national identity with care and concern. If nothing is done today and done fast, the museum pieces that Binam Bikoi talks of may just rot and vanish into the abyss of universalism propelled by the fast-moving engines of globalisation. Maurice Tadadjeu, a memberof the session of 15 May 1985, reacting to Binam's views wonders if there has been no experiment in illustration in the form of films of certain traditional epics. Tadadjeu goes on to say that he has always been impressed by the way the Americans have exploited their tradition. He cites the "Far West" where the fight between the Americans and the Indians has been put in film form so that the little children can understand their history. He suggests that the competent authority should help in experimentation on illustrating certain Cameroonian traditional epics.

This study will be followed by a practical phase on condition that the competent authority, the Ministry of Culture, assists in the realisation of proposed designs. Charles A. Bodunde( ) in an attempt to provide a solution borrows the words of Cyprian Ekwensi and maintains that:

> *The African writer must first look at his own heritage. Then he must look around at what is available to him. If he decides to adapt existing forms to suit his needs, he can still bring to these forms trends of identity and distinction, which will give him a place in the forms known and accepted by the world at large. (24)*

This global vision, for it to be credible or relevant, must be linked to the heritage of indigenous or group culture of the tale before being linked or adapted to existing literary and audio-visual forms that have universal relevance.

According to Tala, "an understanding of the Social and Cultural background of a literary work is fundamental to its aesthetic appreciation". He goes ahead to pinpoint two glaring points about the discussion of orature when he states that: *"That is, it mirrors cultural values and expresses socially accepted ideas. Therefore, in order to understand and appreciate it fully, it must be seen within its cultural, historical and symbolic context"* *(9)*. Like a new historicist, he sees culture as part of a historical process, with storytelling having an important place within oral prose narratives. He proposes a blending of sound, movement, words and visual effects in coming out with a successful piece of orature. The process of redynamisation which this work intends to carry out will blend the sounds, movements, words and visual effects in creating models for the stage, textbooks, cinema, the television and the Internet so that orature can find a place in the elitist homes in cities and urban dwellings of modern Africa.

Dr. Eben, in an interview with this researcher, observes that there is a belief that what comes from outside Africa is better. He fears that if this trend continues, the Western culture will dominate because they have all the scientific gadgets that they use to transmit various aspect of their culture like dress, songs, speech patterns, eating habits cinema and theatre to other parts of the world. He acknowledges the presence of the Ministry of Arts and Culture but observes that not much is being done to preserve the cultural values of Cameroon. In an interview at his Kumba residence, Chief Nkumbe points to the influence of the French culture in the French and English speaking regions of Cameroon. This is seen mostly in fashion, restoration and educational sectors. He also alerts us to the influence of the Nigerian film industry in the country but more apparently in the South West and North Western regions of Cameroon.

Edjedepang-Kogge, acknowledges that the American culture is the culture that exhibits and presents itself more to the people since they have the mass-media and money to infiltrate other cultures. He acknowledges the presence of American culture in the most conservative countries of the world like China, Russia, Taiwan, South Korea and many Arab nations where American music seem to be admired by the younger generation. He cites the example of the "mini-skirts" that came to the towns through television and which penetrated the villages when city dwellers visited them. The marauding influences of tight-fitting trousers and mini blouses parading the streets in urban and local areas today also found passage through the Western media. The aforementioned worries resound on the fact that Cameroon is far from having a cultural identity of its own since it remains a breeding ground for western and other African cultures. Chief M. L. Endeley, in an interview in his palace in Buea, warns that our culture is our identity and if we lose it, we will regret. He appreciated the efforts of this researcher and notes that he is happy that the worry of a cultural degeneration was coming from the younger generation.

The story, *"How a Slave Boy Became a Chief"* centres on inheritance, a cultural concept of importance in most African communities. In Chief Aba's village, where the story is set, inheritance is matrilineal and so Kahle, nephew to Chief Aba, was supposed to be next of kin. Kahle's disrespectful, lazy, dishonest and immoral attitudes make the whole village eager to accept a change in the tradition of chieftaincy succession in the land. The story passes on the following message: a people are the custodians of a culture and may unanimously change it if need be. This flexibility had not been common to many villages of the forests and grassland regions of Cameroon until the corroding influence of money and civilisation set in. In "The Price of Selfishness in Khotoumy" the culture of solidarity and sharing, which has been part of most African societies, is exalted if the village needs the blessings of the gods. This culture has been preserved until recently with the penetration of an individualised western culture marked by greed and selfishness. The trend which poverty, disease and human suffering are taking today may just be a signal that the gods of Africa are angry with the individualistic lifestyles of Africans in the village and urban centres. It also reveals the important place storytelling has in the tradition of Africans as Baba Buhngieh, the storyteller always told the children to be kind to everyone for the gods usually called around for food and water.

These stories, if redynamised and transformed to fit in with aspects of modern technology, will remind Africans of some of those cultural values that assure peace, unity, solidarity and continuity.

Redynamisation in Favour of Peace, Unity and Cooperation

Storytelling remains a vital tool in the resolution of conflicts and differences between individuals, tribes and nations. This is through the values of peace, unity and peaceful co-existence preached in the tales. Do we blame the upsurge of inter-tribal wars, civil strife, inter-state conflicts and terrorism on the downward trend of storytelling in most

African societies? Can storytelling help in reducing conflicts in the world? In an attempt to situate nations within a conflicting atmosphere, Dr. Adamou Ndam Njoya (1985) observes:

> *The history of Nations has always been marked and staked out by egotistical preoccupations with combating others and consequently by the struggle to always assert one's own identity vis-à-vis (of) others, while being ready to destroy the others and assimilate them. (144-145)*

The conflicts that exist, according to Njoya, are products of history due to the very nature of man, aggressive in nature and always in conflict with his fellow man. Redynamising the storytelling event will help in spreading values of peace and cooperation through tales. Most of the tales and songs emphasize aspects of unity, peace and solidarity amongst peoples and nations.

We also observe that we live in a materialistic world which is extremely acquisitive, sinister, and crippled by exploitation, egoism and conflict. In today's African society civil wars, tribal and border conflicts dominate news headlines and blur the vision of hope of Africans working towards peace. The stories chosen for this study are geared towards the creation of an individual who has the weapons of unity, peace and solidarity in a beleaguered and war-torn Africa. The creation of the African Union and other moves towards a global African culture and world view will make the African look above ethnic and tribal lines. Okpewho blames modern poets for not giving enough time to explore possibilities that the tradition may provide a meaningful opening in seeking solutions to contemporary problems. Some of these problems include civil wars, ethnic conflicts, coups d'états, poverty and unemployment. Hans Van Ginkel blames all these aspects on globalisation stating that: *"Le développement du terrorisme international, de sombre perspectives économiques et une déception croissante devant les résultats de la globalisation en particulier dans les pays les moins avancées, sont à l'origine de cette inquiétude grandissante"(75).*

Redynamising storytelling using modern media and the Internet will facilitate an interchange of moral and ethical values from different parts of the world. The Internet will also serve as access to a careful selection of these methods aimed at conflict resolution. The weapons used by the United Nations Organisation (UNO), the African Union (AU) and other peace-keeping bodies in Africa, Europe and America can easily be accessed through the Internet. Tales adapted to serve this vision will easily be reached by decision-makers if a website is created to conserve them. Our study aims at creating a website for the conservation and transmission of various aspects of Cameroonian artistic, and written oral traditions.

Unity and solidarity at individual and family levels has been made easy from time immemorial through storytelling. A number of conflicts between members of the family, relatives and close neighbours have been resolved at individual and village level through the wisdom learned from the stories. At times the settling of disputes between families is presided by proverbs, songs and even anecdotes that reveal aspects that have a link with the problem or problems concerned. Clement Okafor (2004), intimates that modern African nations can adapt their oral traditions to current realities and employ them as effective instruments of civic education especially in an era when the entire world has been transformed into a global village. On this note he states that the mission of such education is to endow the citizens with information and skills to recognize and to do what is right in any given situation. As a tool of national integration, he intimates that:

> *At the present time, one of the most pressing issues that confront many African states is the problem of National integration; many of these recently independent countries have difficulties in weldilng into one state their numerous ethnic nationalities. Fortunately, this handicap can be surmounted through effective civic education programs* (1)

The tale *How the Bafut fought a War Against Themselves* is a glaring example of a tale that hinges on the use of war as a means of dominance and superiority over weaker groups and tribes. The people of Bafut, conscious of their strength and superiority and in a bid to consolidate their position as the strongest tribe in the area, plan to instil fear and terror amongst the Bujongs. Their plan fails and instead of killing the Bujongs, they engage in a bloody battle against their own warriors. It is thanks to the assistance of the Bekaris that their fon is rescued from the hands of the Bujongs. The experience taught them the lesson that war is not a matter of might but an effort characterised by intelligence and tact. They also came to terms with the fact that a weaker tribe has the capacity to defeat a stronger clan. In essence, they learn that war is not a means of exercising superiority over other groups.

It is in this wise that the tale serves as a means of understanding the role and function of power. On this note Graham Furniss and Elizabeth Gunner(1999) state that intentionality brings to the fore the myriad, overlapping types of purpose to amuse, to satirize, to teach, to expound, to warn, and to stir. Furniss and Gunner also affirm that people producing oral literature are not just commentators but are often also involved in relationships of power themselves, in terms of supporting or subverting those in power. According to them, the words and the texts have the ability to provoke, to move, to direct, to prevent, to overturn and to recast social reality. They identify a number of dimensions relative to a complex set of power relations within which the performer, audience and denoted individuals and groups are enmeshed. Firstly, they point to the appropriation of expressive forms by the state and the application by the state, or by corporate organizations or social groups, of oral forms to particular purposes. They point as example, how control is established and maintained and how expressions of resistance or alternative views are articulated, which may lead to praise song transformed into innuendo or vilification. They point a second issue in which oral forms articulate and represent to the performer and audience particular visions of existing power relations in society. According to them, these constitute part of a continuing debate about older versus younger, husbands and wives, mothers and daughters, fathers and sons, one generation and the next, aristocrats and commoners, one ethnic group as against another and elites and ordinary people. A third dimension which they identify revolves around the question of the instrumentality of oral performance in affecting existing power relations. According to them, the focus is upon the ability of performance to transform and not simply to represent existing power relations or to operate across the margins of praise and mockery. The fourth issue, identified by them, concerns the relation of gender and genre, wherein women are constantly redefining the terms by which they are signified within broader social discourses. They cite Duran's essay which explain how the emergence of powerful women singers in Mali has not only shifted power relations within the music industry but has shifted the discourse on gender and enabled women to produce their own signifying terms. Finally, they point to the dynamics of language use in the context of a variety of communicative strategies, related to the wielding of power in society.

The tale also brings us to the reality of orality and the power of the state. Furniss and Gunner, refer to Mlama (1992) who point out the danger of a too unitary notion of nationalism. They point to Mlama who suggests a static and artificial use of nation and culture with the latter rigidly used as part of official nationalist practice. According to Furniss and Gunner, Mlama looks at oral art in relation to the Tanzanian state and its political programme and states that the state proposed a major revaluation and endorsement of a wide variety of indigenous cultural forms, thereby striking a position opposed to the colonial silencing of the people? The case in French Africa is a source of worry. On this note, Mlama decries the monopolistic state control of patronage and the use of art for propaganda and stigmatises government for not having a cultural policy with resources to support art. He expresses surprise at the fact that the artist does not bite the hand that feeds it in spite of the fact that it very rarely gets fed but sees hope in the parallel existence of unofficial art in song and in popular theatre, which attempts to 'empower' the artist and, through the artist, ordinary people. In essence Furniss and Gunner observe that "the Tanzanian example clearly illustrates the way in which issues of 'political correctness' are tightly interwoven into the content and performance contexts of much oral art, and yet oral art has the ability, on occasion, to transform itself out of one political function into another.

They refer to Hofmeyr who examines the interface between native administration bureaucracy and chiefs in south Africa in the period between 1920 and 1950, and points at attempts by the native administration officials to impose the authority of written documentation and appropriate styles of language and the countervailing strategies employed by chiefs and their people to retain many of the distinctive characteristics of orality. They point to the frustration of the native administrative officials who are required to explain verbally, to exemplify verbally and to justify verbally information whose written authority was not accepted by its addressee. They also point to Kofi Agovi who examines the role of *Avudwene,* a particular oral performance in the situation of a public festival in Ghana which evolve around the debate between two classes of people in Nzema society, 'chief me' and 'young men'. According to them, young men dominate the articulation of ideas within 'avudwene' about the way in which chiefs, and other individuals, do behave and should behave and view *'avudwene'* as both a forum for the discussion of constitutional principle and an effective check upon the behaviour of the executive. According to them, Agovi sees proverbs encapsulating values and philosophical positions that are part of general popular sentiment. According to Furniss and Gunner, the deployment of proverbs in the *'avudwene'* is part of the articulation of popular sentiment in public debate by one important class against another which cannot afford to ignore that class.

As a means of representing power relations, Furniss and Gunner refer to Azuonye, who sets out through the representation of kings in Igbo tales, to legitimate authority on the one hand, and the abuse of power on the other. According to them, the dominant ideas centre on positive and negative representations of *'eze'*, which Azuonye generally glosses as 'king' in the tales, but which in society can constitute a 'leader' in a variety of social, political and religious spheres. Furniss and Gunner describe these tales thus:

> *Tales which focus on negative representation tend to follow a pattern in which oppression leads to resistance which leads to a reversal of fortune/ defeat for the oppressor. The tales potray, inter alia, the sadistic king, the jealous king, the king who imitates Benin, the king who is humiliated and the king who does not maintain royal distance. In each of these representations there is the strong presence of the positive alternative set of tales:*

> *the amiable king, the moral king, the firm but fair king, the king who investigates fully, the king who rules by persuasion and not by force, the king whose promises are inviolable and the king who maintains distance"* (9)

They state that for Azuonye, the exemplification of good governance in these tales is centred upon the restrictions upon the behaviour of the king which are the checks of democratic constraint, especially arbitrary, unconstitutional behaviour which are defined through these popular representations.

Oladele Taiwo (1967) while pointing out that oral traditions form an integral part of the culture of any group of people, and reflect the people's way of life, asserts that: *"different versions of the same basic story, which arose spontaneously in various places, can be found in different parts of the world"* (11). According to Taiwo, what happens is that at every stage and with each group the content of the story changes to suit the needs and beliefs of the group. This accounts for the similar variations of tales from the forest and grass fields of Cameroon. Our intention is not to focus on the changing nature of the tale, but to create a version of these tales that is mutually accepted by the different audiences from the diverse cultural backgrounds; as such the tale becomes not only a national cultural marker, but a unifying factor of the different ethnic groups and religions of Cameroon. Also, our interest is that while the tale addresses the needs and beliefs of the group, it should also not leave out the needs of the nation, the world and mankind in general.

Taiwo illustrates this with the story of the "Great Flood" with many versions of the same story all over the world, and affirms that the Yoruba version of the story is different from all other versions because it has a distinct Yoruba colouring and a connection with life which is regarded as the cradle of the Yoruba and Orunmila, one of the most important deities of the Yoruba. He also refers to the example of *Cinderella*, with over a hundred versions. On this note, he recapitulates that: "Although such tales are now told mainly for amusement and entertainment, the version in each region or country reflects local pride, national interests and the traditional way of life"(12-13). He intimates that while we appreciate the international character of oral literature, we should also take into consideration the national and cultural significance attached to it by different racial groups. The adaptation of Tale No 3 permits us to integrate aspects such the role of the game guard acceptable by both Western and African nations today in wildlife and forest protection.

Economic Factors in Favour of Redynamisation

Global economic trends today favour global blocks and conglomerates. Economics, as part of a people's culture, remains the life-wire of the survival of nations, states, cities, towns and even villages in Africa and the world at large. Storytelling is an art that can be used in transmitting economic values while at the same time serving as a source of revenue. Redynamising the storytelling event will attract a monetary value although it may be an expensive project. In the past, it has cost the nations of Africa huge expenditures.

The Ministry of Arts and Culture has put in much and continues to do so in carrying out research on Cameroonian oral tradition. Much revenue is yet to be attracted because the tourism industry is still in its infancy in Cameroon. Our oral tradition remains a veritable gold mine which when exploited will serve as an important source of revenue to the state. S. T. Akindele, T. Gidodo and O. R. Olaopo(2002) of the Department of Political Science, Obafemi Awolowo University decry the changing faces and phases of globalisation with its primary focus of exploiting African resources, disintegrating its economics and incorporating them into international capitalist economy. Since culture is a reservoir of African resources, it is also not left out. They also observe that an increased pace of capital mobility is now shifting prospects for economic development and growth toward a global level. They see this as an indication of the expropriation of surplus and capital from the African economies. This is a glaring and obvious threat but Africans are yet to be threatened with these trends orchestrated by globalisation. Instead, steps should be taken to counteract some of the moves and policies set up for purely economic purposes. One of these steps taken by this researcher involves selecting and adapting African oral narratives that could be exploited in theatres, the movie industry and cartoon production houses, for proliferation to other parts of the world through the television, the Internet, video cassettes and compact discs. The end products will serve as veritable sources of income to all those involved in the transformation process and the state in general.

It should be observed that in the past much was not derived from the arts. Dorothy S. Blair, writing as far back as 1966, in a foreword to *Tales of Amadou Koumba*, observes that one of the activities of the Government sponsored school of Arts and Conservators of Music of West Africa involves sending leading trained troupes of singers and dancers to Europe and America to perform African songs and ballets on stage and on radio. She also observed that griots were used to conserve and transmit the musical and artistic heritage of their people. This kind of exercise involves huge financial sacrifices and risks in the past and even today. With the present liberalisation policies in most countries, coupled with economic crisis, the states of Africa are beginning to decline from such investments whose expenditures outweigh profits. Apart from football, other aspects of African culture are yet to attract much income from home governments. These governments in partnership with other firms, corporations and non-governmental organisations at home and abroad are investing much on the television, the Internet and the radio in order to get to a wider section of the populations. The western world is using these media as avenues for transmitting the cultural and artistic heritages to other parts of the world. Organised concerts in music and dancing are popularised through the television and the Internet. It is only by transforming the oral prose narratives, and other aspects of our oral tradition, into cartoons for the television and the Internet and into recorded songs and African drama and film that they can have easy access to other parts of Africa, Europe, Asia, America. It is only through these means that they could stand the test of globalisation and compete in a world contest of cultures. Successful productions will, no doubt, attract revenue into the Cameroonian and African coffers.

The Therapeutic Value of Redynamising the Oral Tale

Drama is relevant in helping to meet the needs of people and students with learning and physical disabilities, those with behavioural and communication difficulties, sensory difficulties and poor health conditions. Paula Crimmens (2006) defines drama therapy as the use of improvisation, role-play, mime, music and movement, storytelling, masks and rituals, puppetry, theatre games and scripted drama as a therapeutic vehicle. To Crimmens, it builds confidence, increases self-awareness, relaxation and responsibility, and operates on a variety of levels such as physical, emotional, imaginative and social.

Crimmens cites Sue Jennings (1992) who states that drama therapy is a means of bringing about change in individuals and groups through direct experience of theatre art and also the British Association of Drama therapists (BAD) which defines drama therapy as the intentional use of the healing aspects of drama and theatre within the therapeutic process and a method of working and playing which uses action to facilitate creativity, imagination, learning, insight and growth.

The selected stories have a power not only to entertain students with disabilities, but to get them physically involved and active. The smiles and laughter generated in the process of dramatizing the tale have healing and therapeutic dimensions. It is in this vein that Crimmens affirms that many students with a learning disability may become anxious and more distractible in an unstructured environment. The use of traditional stories, according to Crimmens as drama therapy, capture attention with both their content, which is usually exciting, adventurous and sometimes daunting, especially as their structure is predictable and consistent.

It is common in our society to find students with learning difficulties. There are special schools and centres for the blind, deaf and dumb. They are given special attention and care as they follow mainstream academic programmes in the curriculum. Dramatizing the tales using process drama and forum theatre techniques amongst learners with disabilities will enable them build confidence, improve friendship ties, trust and hope in themselves and others around them. It is in this vein that Crimmens affirms:

> As a group-based therapy, drama therapy provides a microcosm of a world that may be too bewilding, over-stimulating and verbal for the learning disabled child to navigate. Poor impulse control impacts on social behaviour and the drama therapy session works to improve this-even just the process of sitting on a chair and awaiting your turn goes some way to teaching impulse. Implying music in the process also yield valuable results. Music to a blind or lame child is not only entertaining but soothing and relaxing. He cites Aldridge, Gustorff and Neugebauer (1995, p.190), who intimate that "music therapy encourages children without language to communicate and has developed a significant place in the treatment of mental handicap in children. (15)

This chapter has demonstrated how redynamising the storytelling event in Africa is a process that will ensure the continuity of moral, didactic, cultural and economic policies in an atmosphere of peace and cooperation in a global village. It will also ease the acquisition of these values by the young, the old, statesmen, local authorities and international bodies that are daily seeking for a peaceful world. Redynamisation will also permit educational establishments, individuals and families to get easy and quick access to available material on African oral tradition through the Internet, television and movies. The process will also lead to the creation of more solid and lasting conservation facilities in the forms of cassettes, video, compact discs, the satellites and hard disks. Members of the urban audience will have an opportunity to come across an array of African oral traditions, which are presently under the custody of rural dwellers.

PART FIVE

Process Drama and Adapting the Cameroonian Oral Tale to a Play in the Classroom

This chapter will focus on the process of adapting the Cameroonian oral tale to play with the aid of adaptation and guided by Process Drama in practice. It will examine the theoretical and practical methods of adapting *Yomandene and the Stubborn Son* into a play script. Focus will be on the choice of the tale, its relevance to the process and aspects such as setting, characterisation, plot structure, dramatic dialogue, and action. Through process drama, we shall examine the outcome of the adaptation process made possible through the contributions of the facilitator or teacher and students in a classroom learning situation. The final tale will be a combination of the role of the playwright as adapting artist, and the students who contributed in reshaping the tale.

<u>Adapting *Yomandene and the Stubborn Son* from Tale to a Play</u>

The process of adapting this version of *Yomandene and the Stubborn Son* from tale to play is intriguing and systematic. By taking the tale from the fireside to the stage, the adapting playwright is in essence attempting to address a wider audience, raise new issues concerning the tale, situating the tale in a wider context and leaving it to a broad/mixed audience for interpretation and analyses.

Pedagogic Applications

The folk tales under study conform to the tastes and sensibilities of the present-day Cameroonian audience. While adapting them, it will be necessary to take into consideration the demands of the learning environment. The tales all contain universal wisdom, warmth and truth. In this section, we are going to apply the tale under classroom environment necessitating the participation of a theatre facilitator, the teacher and students. The process falls under the practice of drama education. Wee Su Jeong (2009) distinguishes between "drama education" and "theatre education' by stating that theatre education deals with an actor's formal performance in front of an audience, where drama education focuses on participants' process of exploration and meaning making.

It is important to conduct the research in a natural setting. It may be a regular classroom or a special drama classroom. There is one key participant, the drama specialist, who works with the teacher and the students. Jeong prescribes a research site which can be a school which provide drama education to young children in an early childhood program or a school where Drama education is taught by a specialist with rich knowledge and experience. In our case, the teacher is a trained Secondary school teacher in English Language and Literature while the participant is a teacher of Drama and Theatre arts at the university level. The techniques of Process Drama were also employed. According to Winston, the term process drama is used currently to describe this type of educational, improvisatory drama, with emphasis on important dramatic learning experiences gotten through the creative processes rather than from within received and distant dramatic products. Winston lists its features which include separate scenic units linked in an organic manner; thematic exploration rather than isolated or random skit or sketch; an event or happening and an experience which does not depend upon a written script; a concern with participants' change in outlook; improvisational activity, outcomes not predetermined but discovered in process; a script generated through action and the learner actively working both within and outside the drama. These qualities, according to Winston, are indicative of drama's open-ended and participatory nature. Winston also proposes the use of archetypes, which according to him, have a strong narrative function within fairy tales as they impact immediately upon children, providing clear and instant recognition patterns. According to Winston, the figures in fairy tales share more in common with the stock characters of popular fiction and with those of popular drama. He quotes O'Neill (1995) who state that:

> *Valuable pre-texts for process drama occur in folk- tales, fairy tales, myths and historical incidents --- myths and archetypes never merely reside in remote and seemingly irrelevant tales of long ago. Their powerful echoes still wait to wake us through the pre-texts we employ. These archetypal and essentially dramatic threads in the*

> *work will connect it with a wider theatre heritage and the literary, mythic and dramatic legacy of other cultures as well as with the soap operas and popular movies, where archetypes clearly persist. (p.43)*

Winston adds further that if archetypal figures enable children to make connections between the particular and the general, then within process drama, the brotherhood code helps children make similar connections in morally expansive ways, able to transform and deepen the archetype. According to him, a thief may come to belong to the brotherhood of all those who resort to crime due to social circumstances; who try to reform their moral actions in vain; who suffer as a consequence of their misdeeds and who eventually believe in the social justice of wealth redistribution.

Winston intimates that the ending of a story drama is as significant as the ending of a story for the values resonated will last longer within us. To this he opined that drama is essentially about problems finding, not problem solving. On this note he affirms that the action must finish and false attempts to finalize it should be avoided. He goes further to state that if we accept that empowerment is a major aim of education, then one of the aims of moral education should be to help children grow into responsible human beings by convincing them that their ethical decisions can make a difference and that some are more justifiable than others.

Winston (1991) goes further to stress that:

> *In our postmodern society, children face a saturation of stories in all kinds of genres and no one, dominant-cultural source can be said to provide them. This confusion can only be exacerbated by the fact that television, video and audio cassette, comics, magazines and books do not provide any opportunities for children to engage in active discourse with their meanings, and hence with their values. As such, rather than being instructive, they are potentially so many 'invitations to incoherence', a phrase applied by Gergen to the postmodern technologies of social saturation (173).*

On selecting schools Winston proposed that it is important to select a variety of local primary and secondary schools not yet exposed to the practice of educational drama ensure that the schools are selected in both rural and urban settings, select both government-funded, private and religious schools and ensure that the classes are grouped to reflect the social and age realities of the learners.

On teaching the lessons and gathering evidence, Winston points out that based on his experience, he wished to work under the same conditions as class teachers, respect their timetable, and do work that reflect the social reality of the everyday primary school classroom. He proposes that teachers gather data that would capture the experience and make it intelligible and susceptible to subsequent analysis and argument, collect raw or interpretive data and immediate or interim data. Raw data, according to Winston, is evidence with no specific interpretative focus at the time it was collected, whereas interpretive data was concerned with evaluative judgements. Immediate data, to him, is that which was gathered at the time the lesson was prepared and taught while interim data was gathered over a period between the teaching and the final written analysis.

Winston lists raw data which include the texts of the stories and directly to inform the lessons and the historical sources of the texts, lesson plans, video and audio recordings of the lessons taught; children's writing or drawing from the sessions or follow up sessions led by the teacher. Winston points out that it is common at this level for children to be requested to keep journals or to record their written responses at the end of the lesson. Winston also proposed that the children be allowed to write in ways they were used to and in ways the class teacher would use to develop the drama ideas in separate sessions through straight forward written questions, story writing, simple poetry, and drawing. Winston found all these difficult and concluded that the best sources of information about individual children's reflections and responses were the whole class discussions recorded on video and audio tape. In our study we used an audio tape recorder to record the tale and the discussions in class. On relevant school documentation, we had to rely on internet facilities provided by the facilitator who doubled as a research student. We consulted the school library but found nothing on drama education.

Winston also provided some guidelines on presenting the findings. These include a summary of the tale and an analysis of the moral values embedded within the text and in the historical sources which have influenced it, an explanation of the focus of the case study, a narrative summary of the lessons with relevant contextual details about the school, the children, the conditions under which the sessions were taught and the reasons behind the choice of focus for the drama including detailed analyses of selected parts of the lessons, intended to throw more light of each case study. In this vein Winston proposes that children act out what they see as an appropriate ending for the story while the teacher explores how children can engage with ethical thinking and express moral meaning through the art form of process drama.

He goes further to identify the children's perceptions of the values in the story by recognizing a wide variety of good and bad behaviours within the context of the story, deconstructs the ethical values embedded in the narrative and to reconstruct the ethics of the story in the light of the sense they made of the characters actions. On this note Winston opines that the choice of focus for the drama was, intended to provide a platform for the exploration of a current moral debate through a situation which acted as a metaphor for these issues. He adds that his intention is not to present drama as a vehicle whose efficacy we judge only in a child's responses outside the art form but to illuminate how drama can enable children to make moral meanings in ways which are distinctive to it.

He also states that while analysing the tale, the learners should be able to work out possible endings of the tale suitable for children of their age in dramatic form, employ forum theatre which sees the teacher speak and act based on the suggestions of the children. The process, he notes, should end with the invention of a new story with new characters and transformed into their home environment with their parents playing active parts. He also recommends that the children should be free to question the school teacher about his or her role referred to as teacher-in-role. He also proposes that teachers inform the children about the source or origin of the tale both religious, social and cultural, help them decide what the moral of the story might be with a number of possibilities, asks them to suggest examples of good ethical conduct in the story and note these down, ask them if the story was a good one for children of their age or younger and whether they thought the ending ought to be changed and put them in groups.

For practical and pedagogic reasons, Form Three of the Cameroonian school system was chosen because it is at this level that critical and analytical skills of learners are developed. The subject chosen is Literature in English and the school is Government Secondary School, Bwiyuku in Buea Sub-division. This researcher played the role of theatre facilitator while Noupea Nkayimbo Margaret was the Literature teacher, playing teacher-in-role while the students played students-in-role.

The facilitator and the teacher opted for the tale of *Yomandene and the Stubborn Son* because of the lessons relevant to the moral and social upbringing of the Cameroonian youths and other young people in Africa and other parts of the world. This choice was motivated by the fact that the oral tale continue to play vital role in the growth and development of young people who live in areas where the storytelling event is vibrant. The oral tale also appeals naturally to children, who can often identify with the characters in the tales and share in the feelings and emotions of the characters. Teachers also exploit the resources provided by the tale to integrate social aspects of the curriculum and relate these issues to societal realities. The oral tale can also be used by the classroom teacher to teach subjects such as English Language, History, Civic and Moral Education, Health Education, Human Rights and Environmental Studies.

Paul Crimmens(2006) presents several reasons for the use of folktales in drama therapy. These are also relevant in other approaches. These include: *folktales provide an existing structure for both the student and facilitator and have a recognizable beginning, middle and end.They provide a host of resources for the facilitator. According to Crimmens, Folk tales, fairy tales and myths form a vast storehouse of material, easy to access, sift through discriminate and choose what best reflects the needs of students.Traditional stories mirror aspect of individuals in the group and affirm their experience; and also affirms a student's cultural identity by the use of a story from his own culture.*

Traditional stories address issues in an indirect way, since they are firmly located in the distant past and long ago period. According to Crimmens, this is relevant to professionals working creativity with students where they are concerned about getting access to unconscious material which they do not feel qualified to deal with. *Working with myth and traditional stories performs the function of distancing and providing emotional safety.* On this note Crimmens states that the student can choose to identify with the characters and their dilemmas or not. *Traditional stories are facilitators for education about values and express issues in ways easily understood by students. In essence the stories enhance harmony, peace and community development.*

<u>The Choice of Students and Class</u>

It is vital to select the group of students who will benefit from the traditional stories. Crimmens suggest groups of developmentally and chronologically younger students. This is so, because traditional stories have a simple structure and narrative, which can teach students about the consequences of actions and help demystify complexities of human behaviour and emotions. Crimmens warns that it is important to be wary about the possibility of triggering past trauma amongst disable students and to avoid scenario close to the students' own experience. Crimmens advises that we devise stories with students who are older or in the adolescent stage of their growth. He provides a series of guidelines for choosing traditional stories as follows:

1. There is plenty of action and less description and dialogue.

2. The action in the story is often constellated around a challenge or task. Crimmens provide six stages of the story structure as follows:

3. Who is the character, animal, creature or thing that this story is about?

4. What is his or her task or goal?

5.   What or who are his or her supports? To Crimmens, this can be external, as in the case of people or animals, or internal, as in the case of personal attributes like courage or steadfastness.

6.   What are the obstacles, the things that stand in the way of achieving the goal?

7.   How is the goal achieved?

8.   What happens next? What is the outcome? Is that the end of the story or does it carry on?

On the use of fabric, masks, and percussion, Crimmens recommends that props need not be expensive. According to him, they can be everyday objects transformed by imagination and a little creative flair. He advises that we choose props according to the students with whom we work. He also recommends that we teach students ground rules about the props. To Crimmens he does not allow students to rummage in the props bag at the beginning of the session. He asks students not to snatch props from one another and to treat them with care. He intimates that sometimes he nominates students to gather up and replace the props in the bag at the end of the session.

In applying the oral tale in any classroom learning environment, the teacher should invite his imagination and those of the students. Both should be involved in a creative learning process that shapes and reshapes their original idea and the outcome of the tale bound on the lesson plan. In order to introduce folk tales to the students, Mike Peterson and Jennifer Hind (2005) recommend that folk tale elements, critical analysis, skill-based instruction, creative writing project, cultural studies, the individual stories in terms of writing, reading, listening and speaking should be considered. Folk tale elements, according to Peterson and Hind are the information and lesson plans about the elements of folk tales, including specific activities and instructional strategies to teach about each of the elements. These include character development, setting, plot and themes. Critical analysis according to them involves teaching students to analyse and interpret folk tales through a critical lens, and also developing an understanding of social development, cultural implications and trends in literature. As far as skill-based instruction, is concerned, they point to the use of folk tales to teach a variety of skills such as decoding, fluency, oral presentation and grammar. The creative writing project, involves the use of folk tales to teach styles of writing such as persuasive, descriptive and narrative in a fun and educational format, such as a newspaper. Cultural studies permit learners to learn more about the various tribes, villages, nations and cultures from which the stories come. The writing, reading, listening and speaking activities of individual stories involve lessons, activities and strategies based on individual folk tales.

Peterson and Hind provide a set of activities whose content and suggested activities are meant to be adapted and modified to suit the needs of the intended audience including younger students who may need additional help in reading and understanding the stories. These can be applied in the teaching of Literature in the Cameroon school system. This precedes basic literary and narrative notions introduced in Forms One and Two. It is usually in form three, that more skills geared towards preparing learners for the General Certificate of Education (G.C.E.) ordinary levels are introduced. Peterson and Hind provide some activities which served as suggestions of how to introduce folk tales to students. These activities have been applied to the tale under study.

Firstly, the teacher wrote the words "folk Tale" on the chalkboard and created a *K.W.L* chart on three columns to discuss the topic. K-refers to 'What you know', W – for "what you want to learn", and L for "what you have learned".

In the application of K on the first column, the teacher asked the students to say what they understood as an oral tale, if they have ever taken part in a storytelling event, who the participants were and when the exercise normally takes place. In applying 'W' on the second column, the teacher referred to the story "Yomandene and the stubborn son". The varied and different responses by the students were written on first and second columns respectively. The third column will be completed after the unit to determine the learning outcomes.

Secondly, the theatre facilitator asked the teacher to dress up as a character from a popular or common folk tale. In this wise the teacher wore a black gown that covered her hands and legs and a mask bearing the face of a wild animal. The facilitator then asked the students to identify what was in front of them. Some of them identified the beast as a Hippopotamus while others identified it as Rhinoceros. The students were also influenced by the movement and the strange and coarse words and sounds that it uttered.

Thirdly, the teacher displayed other oral tale books and asks students to name the genre that is common for all the books. The learners identified prose as the most common genre. The tale under study was classified as a fairy tale for children. In this vein, the teacher created a folk tale survey in order to discover what they already know about oral tales. The teacher used survey information from the whole class to create a graph to display the responses. Some of the responses got include:

Oral tales are stories of the past narrated to us in the evening by our parents.

Oral tales are stories about the great deeds of our ancestors.

Oral tales are fairy tales told by way of mouth recounting the activities of animals, man and supernatural human beings.

Oral tales are short stories about animals and human beings.

The students were asked to identify the best response. With the aid of the teacher, the third response was adopted to be closer to the correct definition of the oral tale.

<u>Graph</u>

Based on these responses, the students were told that a unit on folk tales will be introduced to them. They were assigned to use the internet to gather information on at least one fact about oral tales. This was to enable them write an index card and create a folk tale tree of facts. This was a take-home assignment since most of the students do not own personal lap top computers. The students were also assigned to write the information gathered on index cards provided to them by the teacher. Each of them was given three index cards.

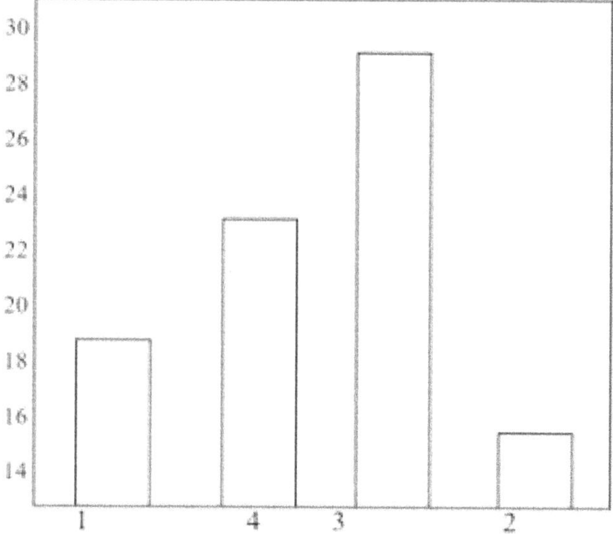

During the next class the teacher introduced the lesson and asked students to recall some of the activities carried out during the previous lesson. He then asked them to hand in their index cards based on the assignment handed to them in previous class.

From the cards, the following were registered about folk tales.

1. Oral tales are stories handed down by the older generation to the younger mainly by way of mouth.

2. Oral tales are myths, legends, and human interest stories narrated by telling.

3. An oral tale is a popular story that we passed on in spoken form, from one generation to the next.

4. Usually, the author is unknown and there are often many versions of the tale.

5. Folk tales comprise fables, fairy tales, legends, and even urban legends.

6. It is a tale or legend originating among a people or folk, especially one forming part of the oral tradition of the common people.

7. Any belief or story passed on traditionally, especially one considered to be false or based on superstition.

8. Oral tales originally began as stories told by word of mouth.

9. All oral tales have a moral lesson to teach.

10. Many oral tales explain how something came to be. These are 'creation myths.

11. Characters in oral tales are usually animals or people.

12. Usually, a character in an oral tale must face a difficult test.

13. Oral tales are usually narrated in the evening.

14. The narration is usually accompanied by song, dance, riddles and proverbs.

Students were assigned to come up with a tree of facts based on arranging the points in order of preference.

The next activity was on character development.

Firstly, students were assigned to categorize each of the characters by traits and types. The following character profile chart was established.

Character Profile Chart

Name of story " Yamandene and the Stubborn Son"

Character name: Yomandene, the Beast	Description of Appearance: scary, wild, frightening, dark in complexion, long nails and fingers, large head, bright eyes.
Picture of Character: *provide Drawing* Image of character reminds me of aliens from the moon.	

Students were also told to complete a character development list referred to as Biopoem. This is to enable them build character accurately.

Character Development BioPoem

1st Line:	Character's name
2nd line:	"It means… " List 3 adjectives to describe the character
3rd line:	"It is the number…" pick any number that reminds you of the character.
4th line:	"It is like"… Pick a colour that reminds you of the character. Do not name the colour rather describe it.
5th line:	"Relative of or friend of…" Name one to three people related to the character.
6th line:	"who does…" Name something unique the character does.
7th line:	"Who has…" Name something unique the character possesses.
8th line:	"who fears…" Name something the character fears.
9th line:	"who wants…" Name something the character wants or needs.
10th line:	"Resident of…" Name the location where the character resides or describe the setting.

Story Title: "Yomandene and the Stubborn Son"

1st line:	Mokosso
2nd line:	Mokosso is rude, impolite and unforgiving
3rd line:	It is the number 3
4th line:	Mokosso is dark in complexion
5th line:	Son of Pa Lyonga and Ma Lyonga and Sasse's elder brother
6th line:	Mokosso insists that his brother goes to the Beast's forest and brings back his missing arrow
7th line:	Mokosso is unforgiving
8th line:	Mokosso fears nobody
9th line:	He wants to get back his younger brother's singing bird and also to get rich and wealthy
10th line:	Mokosso is resident in a house on the farmland near the forest

Story Title: "Yomandene and the Stubborn Son"

1st line:	Sasse

2nd line:	He is kind, polite and obedient
3rd line:	1
4th line:	He is light in complexion
5th line:	Son of Pa and Ma Lyonga and brother of Mokosso
6th line:	He braves all the odds to go into the Beast's village in search of his elder brother's arrow.
7th line:	He is respectful and helpful to the old woman he meets on his way.
8th line:	He fears the beast and the beast's relatives
9th line:	He wants to get back his elder brother's arrow
10th line:	He lives in a hut on the farmland near the forest

On plot development, the teacher employed the Bookmark Strategy, proposed by Peterson and Hind, to remember the plot of the story. In this wise, the teacher with the aid of the facilitator created four bookmarks of equal size. The students were handed four bookmarks to record specific information on each bookmark including the place where the story is set.

In Bookmark 1, the students are instructed to write or sketch something about the part of the text that was most interesting.

In Bookmark 2, they are instructed to write or sketch something confusing.

In Bookmark 3, they are asked to write a word the whole class should discuss, and look up for its definition in a dictionary.

In bookmark 4, the students are instructed to note a favourite quote, word, or image.

The different bookmarks were later collected by the teacher and the facilitator. The different responses are read out to the hearing of all. From these responses the teacher, students and facilitator finally agreed on the following to be included in the master bookmarks.

Below is bookmark strategy based on the aforementioned.

BOOKMARK 1

> The most interesting part of the story is when Sasse succeeds to get hold of the missing arrow and escapes without being hurt.

BOOKMARK 2

> When the beast approaches, Sasse is blinded by the light from his eyes and so picks up his brother's arrow to shoot at the beast.

BOOKMARK 3

> A Beast: Defined by the Collins Online English Dictionary as "any animal other than man, especially a large wild quadruped.

From this definition, the students wanted to know if all animals in the forest should be considered as beasts. The teacher made it clear that all wild animals capable of predating on other animals and human beings should be considered as beasts. This dispelled the pre-concerned notions that they held that beasts were supernatural wild animals from the wild that were beyond destruction.

BOOKMARK 4

> OLD WOMAN: "My dear son, as you move on, your path will become clearer. Nothing will stand before you as obstacle. Your eyes will be brighter to see well".

This was a favourable quote from the tale's adaptation because it was the source of the blessing Sasse got from the old woman due to his obedience and respect of elders.

The quote reminds the students of the blessings that await them when they respect their elders in society.

As an assignment, students were asked to use drawings to retell the events of the story. They were asked to create panels and place one drawing in each panel. They were also asked to write a particular statement describing each panel. They were asked to add dialogue in balloons or bubbles.

They were also supposed to number each panel or frame in order.

In the next class, the teacher and the facilitator assist students to form six groups comprising five students each. They are assigned to discuss the plot development leading up to the ending with the aid of the comic strips. The groups were given twenty minutes to accomplish the task. While they worked, the teacher and facilitator visit each group to see what the students were doing and to assist them where they had difficulties. After this exercise, each group leader read his or story to the hearing of all. A period of ten minutes was reserved for discussion and feedback. With the feedback from students, the teacher and the facilitator, a chronological sequence retelling the events of the story was adopted thus:

1. Pa Lyonga and wife live in a house on their farmland near the forest.

2. In the forest there lived a scary wild beast.

3. One morning, Pa Lyonga's sons, Mokosso and Sasse discover that the grass and trees that were cleared the previous day had all grown back.

4. They report the strange happening to their parents and Pa Lyonga advises them to go back to the farm and watch what happens to the cleared portion of the farm.

5. That same night, they obeyed their father and hid themselves in a thick shrub near the farm. Before

leaving for the farm, Pa Lyonga hands them a poisoned arrow each to shoot and kill the beast.

6.   They wait and finally fall asleep

7.   At midnight, Sasse is woken by the footsteps of the beast and a loud noise as it approaches the farm.

8.   Sasse sees the beast approaching with fiery eyes, mistakenly picks up Mokosso's arrow and shoots at it. The arrow hits the beast on its forehead and sticks on it. The beast retreats in pain with the poisoned arrow.

9.   Mokosso gets up and realizes that his arrow is nowhere to be found. Sasse narrates to him what he had seen and how he had mistakenly used his brother's arrow to shoot the beast.

10.   Mokosso insists that Sasse brings back his arrow.

11.   At home, Sasse reports what had happened on the farm and the missing arrow.

12.   Sasse pleads for forgiveness. Pa Lyonga and wife also plead with Mokosso to forgive his younger brother. But Mokosso insists that Sasse goes out in search of his arrow.

13.   Sasse decides to go to the beast village to search for the missing arrow.

14.   On his way to the forest, he meets an old woman with wounds all over her body living alone in a hut in the forest.

15. Sasse is happy to meet the old woman and considers her his new mother.

16. Old woman blesses Sasse and wishes him success in his quest.

17. Sasse meets another old woman living in a hut covered with weeds and shrubs.

18. Sasse helps her clear the grass on the hut. The old woman also blesses him and advises him that when he arrives the beast's village, he should pretend to be missing.

19. He is led to the beast's compound.

20. He is welcomed by the beast's children as their missing brother.

21. He finds the missing arrow, steals it and escapes. 21- He is chased by villagers from the beast's village.

22. He meets the old woman having wounds all over her body and hides in her hut.

23. The people give up their chase because of the odour coming out of the woman's body.

24. On leaving, Sasse is handed an egg by the old woman and told to break it when he gets to the village. He is also given a nightingale.

25. In the village he breaks it and a mansion appears.

26. Mokosso becomes jealous when he sees the beautiful building.

27. The villagers, thrilled by the singing bird, give Sasse money and precious gifts.

28. Sasse leaves the bird with Mokosso and asks him to take good care of it. Mokoso throws the bird into the air and it flies away.

29. Sasse returns and asks Mokosso to look for his bird.

30. Mokosso proudly leaves for the process hoping to find the bird and also to be blessed with riches.

31. Mokosso meets the old woman with sores on her body and insults her a barren witch. The woman curses him with death.

32. He comes across the woman living in the hut covered with weeds and mocks her. She also curses him.

33. He gets to the beast's village and searches everywhere for the bird.

34. He is killed by the angry villagers.

35. The bird returns to the village and Sasse gets richer.

As a follow-up exercise geared towards building the practical skills of the students, the teacher drew the inverted pyramid proposed by Peterson and Hind and assigned the learners to chart a story and to frame their own thoughts for the story.

A Sketch of the Inverted Pyramid

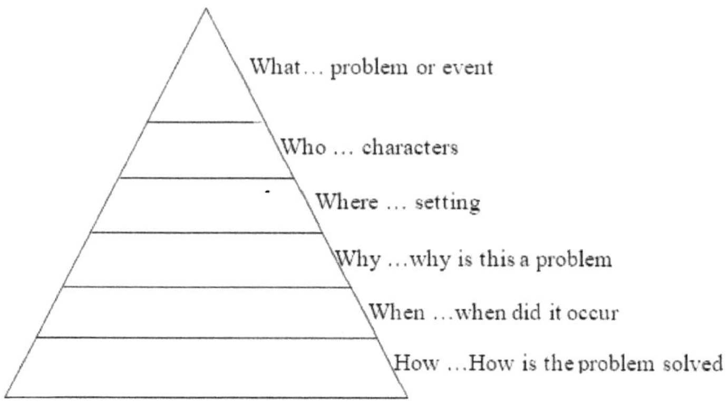

It is important to note that such a lesson was realized in three different teaching periods of an hour each. It also saw the active participation of the teacher, the theatre practitioner and the students in realizing the project.

Citing O'Neill (1994), he points out that successful drama teachers guide, rather than direct, are capable of working with others, consider the opinions of others and freely offers their own ideas. He also adds that teachers need to invite children to create and maintain the dramatic world, through the use of open-ended questions, animated expressions, and enthusiastic responses to the children's ideas. On this note Jeong affirms that this process involves the co-construction of an emergent story that requires the teacher to adopt various roles such as motivator, guide and artist.

Community Awareness and Communication Application

The tale under adaptation serve as veritable weapons of community awareness and communication. Apart from conscientising, they can educate the population on different socio-cultural, economic aspects relevant to society's growth and development. In this we are going to exploit the radio play within the context of educating the Audience on issues relevant to their growth and development. Issues surrounding community awareness include love, peace, harmony, conflict prevention, love for nature and animals and unity. Working with Radio Bonakanda, a radio station situated in Bonakanda, a village on the outskirts of Buea, we engaged in the process of Adapting *Yomandene and the stubborn Son* to a radio play destined for the sensitization of the inhabitants of Buea and its environs.

Radio plays are important not only in communicating what the artist has in mind but in preserving the dialogue and action for future generations. The British Broadcasting Corporation (B.B.C) online guide on "how to write a radio play" describes the radio as an extraordinary medium that can travel through time and space, between centuries and continents. It also intimates that the play can take place in an aeroplane, down a gold mine, on a ship and in someone's mind with the aid of sound alone. It quotes the views of award- winning radio dramatist Mike Walker, who states:

> *Television, for example, never does science fiction very well because it can't afford the production values that are required, whereas with radio you really do have a theatre as large as the universe in*

> *that sense. You're using the muscle of the listener's imagination – they're doing the work with you – and I think that's absolutely terrific". (1)*

Guided by well selected characters, dialogue, sound effects, music, pauses and even silence, the radio play can address a wider audience. It is for this reason that the radio was chosen as an important medium for community sensitisation and education. The proliferation of radio stations is a motivating factor. A case in point is Radio Bonakanda in Buea sub-division which broadcast in Bakweri, pidgin and English. This provides a greater majority of people living in that community to listen to radio plays and to participate in the production process.

The purpose for adapting the tale to a radio play was motivated by the role played by local radio stations as far as education is concerned. We also observed that there are many *Yomandene* tales and different versions that dwell on different topics. The messages inherent in these tales have the power to moralise and conscientise the youths whose actions have an impact on peace, unity and development on a community. For example, an irresponsible and lazy youth is no doubt a hindrance to the development of any community. After discussing with some of the journalists of Radio Banakanda, we saw the need to adapt some of the tales into radio plays which will be produced to assist in the education and moral re-armament of the youth in Buea and it is environs. We also realised that since our target audience comprises mostly of primary and secondary school pupils and students, we opted to adapt the tales in English. As a community radio, the station manager also pointed out that the tales will also be useful to the parents of these kids and a majority who can hardly read or write. So, we agreed that the production in *Mokwe,* the language spoken by the Bakweris, of the same version, could also be realised using people who master the language. But for the purpose of this study the version being proposed is in English.

Below is a proposed radio play version of the tale: N° 1.

SCENE I

(In Pa Lyonga's thatch hut. The silence is interrupted by the chirping of birds in their nests, the barking of a dog, the mating noises of cats, and a hawk screeching. The noise of an iron file rubbing against a cutlass could be discerned)

PA LYONGA

My dear sons, I am an old man now. I fought during the 2nd World War before retiring to this village where I met your grandmother. Since then she has been the flesh of my flesh and bone of my bone. Since your grandparents travelled to the land of our ancestors, your mother has been doing all to make me happy and to see that your stomachs are always full. (hitting *his walking stick on the ground*). She is an angel in human form. I pray you find a wife like her. Before I forget, make sure the farmland is cleared for planting. (*the noise produced by the iron file dominates the silence*)

SASSE

Grandpa, whenever we clear the shrubs, and cut down the branches of the trees, we are surprised that after a day all the grass we cleared has stood on their feet.

PA LYONGA

It's your place to find out the cause of such a strange happening and to seek for a solution.

(The noise of his iron file sharpener gets louder as the teeth of the arrows are filed harder. The hooting of an owl could be clearly heard)

SASSE

Thank you great one! You remain our role model and guide.

SCENE 2

In the forest, the silence is dominated by the chirping of crickets and barking of the dog)

MOKOSSO

Let me clean my eyes. What am I seeing? Hope this is not the beast.

SASSE

Let me also wipe my eyes. Hope this is not a monster.

MOKOSSO

I will shoot anything I see.

SASSE

Even Yomandene?

MOKOSSO

Even Lucifer!

(a loud noise is heard as the beast moves through the shrubs. Silence)

YOMANDENE

(Chanting)

Mauja, Mauja Temeke Jinja

(the voice grows louder and clearer)

Mauja, Mauja

Temeke Jinja

SASSE

Are we safe? Hope we will not be killed?

MOKOSSO

Let's hold our hands so that we can remain alert to see the monster when it finally arrives.

SASSE

Let's rush home before we are eaten by this monster.

MOKOSSO

What are these arrows meant for?

(*there is tremor as the beast moves closer to the farm*)

SASSE

(*Searching for his arrow in his bag*)

Where is my arrow? I must put an end to the life of this beast. Thank God, I found it.

(*saying a little prayer*)

God of the sky and of the land

God of my parents and grand-parents Give me the strength to kill this beast

(He points his bow at the beast and shoots it)

Mokosso, I hit it; I hit it on the head!

BEAST

(*screaming and shouting*)

At last a mortal hit me on my head. This is surely my end!

(*Mokosso is snoring*)

SASSE

Mokosso, get up, we are safe, we are free!

MOKOSSO

Yes, brother. I'm not sleeping.

(*fumbles in his bag and searches for his arrow*)

Sasse, where is my arrow? Hope you didn't use it to shoot the beast?

SASSE

Oh! No! This is my arrow lying on the ground. Brother, in confusion, I mistakenly used your arrow to shoot the beast. I'm sorry brother

MOKOSSO

You must bring back my arrow. I'm not going to forgive you this time

SASSE

The beast went back into the forest with your arrow stuck on its forehead

MOKOSSO

Then you'll have to go to its forest and look for my arrow. Let's report the good news to our parents. (*they rush home*)

SCENE 3

SASSE AND MOKOSSO

(*Panting and breathing heavily*)

Papa, Mama, we saw the Beast. We saw the monster. It has over a hundred eyes on its head. When it opened its mouth, fire came out.

MOKOSSO

(panting)

Great One, it's a monster from hell. We have never seen it before, even in our dreams.

PA LYONGA

(*laughing and coughing*)

It is the great beast that has been with us since creation Mother of the orphans---

MA LYONGA

(*pounding boiled cocoyams*)

Husband of the widows, I will see you shortly.

What great wind lifts the feathers covering the fowl's anus?

PA LYONGA

Come and listen to your young warriors

MA LYONGA

My ears are wide open.

PA LYONGA

Tell your parents what happened to the beast

MOKOSSO

Sasse shot it on the head with my arrow

SASSE

It was out of confusion. I'm sorry

PA LYONGA

Why are you sorry?

SASSE

Because Mokosso wants me to bring back his arrow

MA LYONGA

Mokosso, Mokosso, forgive your brother!

MOKOSSO

I can't forgive him; he must look for my arrow.

PA LYONGA

Sasse is your younger brother, forgive him

SASSE

I will look for his arrow in the beast's forest tonight.

It is important to note the use of words and sound in the stage directions that describe the action or any other activity in the story. This is different from the stage play which relies on stage directions to explain the action. In scene one, the setting is visible thanks to the sounds made by the insects, birds, cats and the dogs. This tells the listener that the action is taking place in a rural area. In most rural areas, the possession of a dog is not for home security but for hunting. So, mention of a dog tells us that its owner should be a hunter or farmer. This is true in the forest and grass field regions where the inhabitants, mostly farmers employ the use of dogs for hunting and guarding them while in the farm.

In scene 2, instead of relying on words on the stage direction to indicate the approach of the beast, we instead use dialogue to indicate this. It is from what Sasse says that we learn that the beast has been hit on the forehead. In a stage play, this action will be clearly expressed in the stage direction. This is to say that in radio script writing, stage directions that does not employ the use of sound, pauses and even silence, are not necessary to be included on the script.

It is also important to note that the message of the story is as relevant as its medium of communication. Such a message can be brought out clearly through concise dialogue which is less verbose. In this wise, the characters are supposed to express what they intend for the audience through words. The following dialogue enables us to get a clear image of the action in the scene.

SASSE

Are we safe? Hope we will not be killed?

MOKOSSO

Let's hold our hands so that we can remain alert to see the monster when it finally arrives.

In a stage play, the aforementioned action will appear thus:

SASSE

Are we safe? Hope we will not be killed?

MOKOSSO

(*Holding Sasse's hands*)

Let's remain alert to see when the monster finally arrives

From the aforementioned, we learn that Sasse holds Mokosso's hands in the stage direction. Below we see the relevance of words in dialogue in revealing action.

SASSE

(*Searching for his arrow in his bag*)

Where is my arrow? I must put an end to the life of this beast. Thank God, I found it.

(*Saying a little prayer*)

God of the sky and of the land

God of my parents and grand parents

Give me the strength to kill this beast

(*He points his bow at the beast and shoots it*)

Mokosso I hit hit it; I hit it on the head!

From the above, we learn that Sasse has found the arrow from what he says. In a stage play such a discovery will be clearly explained in a stage direction thus:

"Where is my arrow? I must put an end to the life of this beast.

(*finding it*)

Thank God!

The radio play is relevant because it will help diffuse a host of lessons and messages in the tale. Kindness is one of the virtues which the story passes across. Mokosso, Sasse's elder brother expresses acts of wickedness when the latter mistakenly uses his arrow to shoot the beast. He would not forgive his younger brother until his arrow is recovered. The message herein is that we should be able to forgive those who mistakenly misplace any of the things we love and cherish. From the story we learn that wickedness is punished while kindness, respect of elders and compassion rewarded. Sasse, in spite of the difficulties finds Mokosso's arrow and in the process, he is rewarded while Mokosso, who finds himself in a similar situation is cursed, and dies in the process of searching for Sasse's singing bird.

The notion of respect is clearly brought out in the story, especially respect for elders. Sasse's respect and care over the old woman earns him her blessings and advice on how to escape the wrath of the beast while struggling to recover the missing arrow. It is thanks to the old woman's advice that Sasse not only recovers the missing arrow but becomes blessed with a mansion. His wicked brother Mokosso who disrespects and abuses the old woman ends up being killed by the beast. This message is relevant in our society today where the youth are so disrespectful of elders, especially old men and women in their vicinity who are usually considered as wizards and witches. In a society where the old are neglected, abused and left to die at home, this tale becomes relevant. It teaches us that though they are old, they remain the custodian of wisdom necessary in liberating mankind from death and leading man on to success. They also have the capacity to bless or curse anyone who extends a hand of kindness and wickedness respectively.

All such messages can be passed across to a greater number of people using radio as a medium. Apart from listening to news, items and other educational programmes, the tales will provide another window for the people to learn from the wisdom of the tales. The radio production process either in cassettes, CD ROMS, flash disks, are veritable means not only transmitting the tales but preserving the tales for the present and future generations.

From the chapter above we have analysed a host of considerations that facilitate the preservation and transmission of the tale in both rural and urban settings and the different areas where the tale either in its original or adapted form can be practically applied to contribute to society's growth and development. Situated in an eco-culture setting, for example, we saw the birth of a new tale that put the environment above individual and selfish ambitions. We also saw the tale at the service of teaching and learning activities geared towards empowering the youths. In essence we saw how the radio play can be vital in disseminating important values and norms to a wider audience.

In this section I have demonstrated practically how the oral tale can be adapted to a play with the aid of building scene, characterization and dialogue. I have also shown how a tale can be lifted from a micro to a macro setting with the possibility of addressing universal issues of pride, harmony and respect of elders. We have also seen how the classroom teacher, with the aid of a theatre facilitator, can adapt the tale in the classroom with the contribution of the learners to teach different aspects of the lesson. We have demonstrated how the oral tale can be transformed to radio plays as a means of reaching out to a wider section of the community.

Conclusion and the Way Forward

Based on the aforementioned theoretical and practical aspects, the oral tale can only be revived, sustained and preserved if its audience provides fertile grounds for its growth and survival. The role of this book in redynamising the tale can only bear fruits if there is a constant effort at creating, narrating and adapting the tales by the relevant actors, in relevant quarters and before a relevant or useful audience. The study analysed the different fieldwork techniques, theories and critical approaches relevant in redynamising the oral tale in an era of globalization. It also reviewed the texts under transformation through a process of adaptation. The study also reviewed related contributions made by scholars and artists on adapting stories, plays and films into other forms of the audio-visual media. Secondly, it focused on the moral, cultural, pedagogic, economic, and therapeutic justifications of transforming the oral tale in an era of rapid cross-cultural exchange and technological advancements. Justifications were also premised on the notions of peace, unity and cooperation in a world crippled by conflict, environmental degradation and immorality. These views were backed by ideas from scholars, traditional authority and persons interested in seeing the oral tale reach its destined audience. Thirdly it situated the historical perspective of moving from tale to play, provided a background to adaptation and practically demonstrated how the selected tale could be effectively transformed to a stage play. This process was made possible by a study of the background of the adapting artist, the reasons for the choice of the play, adjusting the title, stage directions, defining the plot, creating dialogue, creating and adjusting characters, defining the structure of the play and the writing process of the play. By the end of the adapting process, a new play was created that addressed universal values of love, peace, respect and harmony.

From the discussion and viewpoints raised in the preceding chapters, our arguments have been summarized as follows. One of the glaring issues around the importance of the tale in an area of cross-cultural dialogue is the importance of preservation and the demands of transmission and propagation and the extent to which the oral tale can compete with tales in other parts of the world while exploiting the same audio-visual information and communication technological outfits at its disposal. I also raised the issue of an invaluable place of the oral tale in an era where different nations of the world are struggling to export not only goods and services, but also aspects of their culture, to other parts of the world with the intention of not only disseminating their cultural values but implanting these values and practices in different parts of the globe.

The study has led us to some findings. Firstly, at the level of the educational sector, it was realized that the tales if transformed into valuable teaching aids can play a very useful role in the teaching and learning process. I realized that through Process Drama, the gap between the teacher and the student can be bridged thereby leading to effective communication in the classroom. We also discovered the importance of role-play as a teaching technique in the hands of the teacher. This involves inviting students to play the role of animal in front of the class. Secondly, it was discovered that the process of adaptation for stage becomes useful not only to the adapting artist but to the theatre producer, and director and technical crew staging the play. The proposed settings, dialogue and characters created by the adapting artist therefore become not only a guide to the director and technical crew, but also a creative process that reveals the movement from the fireside to the stage.

A main feature of the tales under adaptation is their didactic and moral values. Most of the tales collected touch on moral aspects of the growth and development not only of Cameroonians but to other peoples of the world. In the selected tale we find that the relevance of love, kindness and respect of elders are sine qua non to the harmony, growth and development of any community. In the tale, we learn that the theme of Love, forgiveness, kindness and respect are raised simultaneously. This tale is therefore rich in all aspects that hold and bind human relationships. In the tale, the younger brother who suffers from the hatred of his elder brother is a replica of the conflict existing in most homes today. Even the ultimate success of the younger brother provokes a lot of jealousy in the heart of the elder brother. The younger brother is rewarded because of his respect for the old widow while the elder brother suffers and dies because of pride and disrespect of older persons. From the tale, we discover that respect of parents and other older persons are sources of blessing and success.

This study provided an opportunity for me to make contributions to knowledge. On adapting tales to plays, I demonstrated how a particular tale could be transformed to address not only the issues raised by the narrator in the tale, but other issues which are relevant to different audiences in different parts of the world. I also pointed out the relevance of participation through discussion, feedback and proposals by different members of the audience in the transformation process. I went ahead to prove that a tale can serve as source material and an invaluable cultural heritage that meets the needs and aspirations of the present generation. In this wise, a tale that was intended to serve a purely moral purpose, could be transformed to address an environmental and global concern. I demonstrated such flexibility by employing creativity while adjusting aspects such as plot, characterization, diction, title, stage directions, script treatment, pages and panels respectively. The study can also serve as a guide to budding play, film and comic strips writers and producers interested in oral and other cultural data in writing and producing for stage, cinema and cartoons respectively. At the end of each process, I proved how the birth of a new tale can be achieved which not only serve the need of a particular audience but different peoples in other parts of the world. With the aid of practical examples based on semiotics, new historicism and the performance context approach instructed by drama education and process drama, new and adapted forms of the tales have been created to address global and universal concerns such as morality, conflict and the protection of the environment and wildlife.

Based on the aforementioned benefits, we recommend that at state and institutional levels, there should be a policy that regulates, guides and encourages the production of intangible cultural data into stage plays, movies and cartoons respectively. In this wise, we shall have accomplished the task of preserving the oral tale into concrete images for the entertainment industry. The association of images to the scripts will therefore render the tale more dynamic and interactive. We also recommend that parents create time during the evening to narrate tales to their children as a form of teaching and conscientisation. To those in urban settlements, the weekends can provide valuable time for storytelling and communication. The Ministry of Basic Education and the Ministry of Secondary Education in Cameroon should include storytelling and drama education at their respective levels. This will enable learners master the basics of acting and role play before entering the University. Role play should be reinforced as a basic didactic tool in the teaching and learning process. The national and local radio stations should be equipped with audio visual recording devices for the recording of radio plays based on tales and other common interest stories. These tales accompanied by riddles, jokes and proverbs will enrich the Cameroonian cultural landscape. Storytelling competitions should be organized at local, school and national levels with commendable prizes that attract competitors. These sessions should witness the participation of great storytellers either as judges or competitors. Winners of such competitions at local level can participate at the national level. At this stage the competition should be televised to let viewers all over watch the activities. This will ignite the lost interest in a host of storytellers who feel neglected and abandoned. Some tales can be written on walls or some spaces of museums, monuments, palace walls and other public spaces to remind the public about important events and contribution of heroes. These can be accompanied by graffiti, drawings and illustrations to beef up the wordings. A process of collecting, transcribing and recording the tales should be carried out with the assistance of the Ministry of Arts and Culture, local and international NGO's involved in preserving the intangible cultural heritage of Cameroon. With the aid of a web-page the stories can be preserved for present and future access by students, researchers and lovers of culture all over the world. Bards and narrators should be recognized as their counterparts in music and sports. They should be encouraged and supported through clubs and associations formally created and supervised at local and national levels. Above all the creation of new tales should be encouraged at all levels. In these wise creative writing competitions should be organized to encourage the writing of new tales based on the cultural evolution of the society. This will build our heritage memory and reduce the past. These competitions can be organized based on current themes such as environmental protection, conflict resolution, cross-border criminality, brain-drain, inter- marriages, the relationship between man and animals, human rights and justice. Associated with lucrative prizes, winning tales can be published and preserved for future generations. This will be to remind the present generation that creativity does not die with the narrators or the past.

At a pedagogic level, teachers, especially at the basic and secondary school levels, should be practical and be able to use sketches and plays in class and outdoors. At the University level, research and regular fieldwork should be encouraged. This will bring them closer to the oral sources and the local artists who may be traditional poets, musicians and performers. There is also need for the oral artist to work closely with teachers, comic artists, dramatists and producers. Storytelling should be introduced as a subject in nursery and primary schools while oral literature and theatre arts should be part of the Literature syllabus in high schools. In this same vein, the curriculum in the Government Teacher Training Colleges should include the teaching of the arts especially storytelling and elementary theatre arts. The skills and techniques acquired can be applied to the teaching of any subject in the curriculum. With the introduction of subjects as citizenship, health education, human rights and environmental education, the teacher can currently use storytelling techniques and the role-play method to teach any aspects with the aid of colourful story books on any of these topics. The teacher can be able to draw the attention of the students not only to the words or dialogue but to pictures and illustrations and visuals that enable them see and relate to what they read. The contribution therefore of words and visual elements enables the students not only to recall what they have read or heard but to match the words to the images in real life situations. It is in this light that Tala (2012) suggests that we follow the advice of Oyekan Owomoyela (1989-414) who advocates that folklore in all its ramifications should be a central part of the educational curriculum, and a mandatory subject for all.

Role play, through process drama, should also be encouraged not only as a method of teaching but as an area of training of teachers. With the aid of process drama, the teacher successfully passes across any message with the contribution, participation and suggestions of the learners. By so doing, the learners also contribute to the creation of knowledge and this makes them feel like useful members of the community. With an element of compensation or reward, the individual students that excel will feel proud and encouraged to contribute more. Process drama therefore reduces the gap between the teacher and learner; and renders the teaching and learning process not only exciting but fulfilling. It also sharpens and broadens the student's talent and encourages participation and team work. In order to render the tales more effective as a teaching tool, a story bank can be created which contains story books from the different cultures of Cameroon and Africa in general. The stories can be translated into some national languages especially the language spoken in the area where the school is located with the use of common objects such as masks, traditional costumes, instruments such as drums, gongs, flutes, pianos and guitars for sound effects.

I recommend that apart from plays, the tale can also be acted out as children theatre in schools and other spaces in the community. With the assistance of a theatre practitioner, the children can be called upon to re-enact the tale with the aid of pantomime associated with animal costumes and masks. With the aid of these costumes the children and their facilitators will be able to dramatize the tale in class and even in front of an audience. These will not only enable them speak, walk and gesticulate like the animals being imitated, but they will also empathise with the animals in real life situations. This exercise can be televised or videotaped for rediffusion over television and /or stored in DVDs. On film production, Cameroonian film producers can extract salient aspects of the tale to build the stories of their film scripts. Rather than adapting the tale into film, an important aspect of the story can be introduced into the plot to build the movie. With the aid of flashback, a scene of the war between the people of Bafut can be adapted into a modern story on land conflict. In an interview which I conducted with Thilo Grimm, Coordinator of Photography and Video Workshop in Folkwang University of the Arts in Essen, Germany, Grimm states:

> *Because we are constantly or currently working more and more with video cameras, most photographic cameras can also make small movies. The whole process has become a lot cheaper which means that most PCs or max machine you work on already has software installed. If you go for a small movie, you can normally do it without further investment. There are photographic cameras costing 100 Euros or so and they already can make movies and then you take these films and work with them on a computer. You edit them, you put them together and at the end, you can have a flash movie so you can put in on U-tube or in other parts of the internet. Off course, the sky is the limit, as they say because with investment, you can easily*

spend a lot of money on a better camera which has better lenses, a PC or max which are expensive. Of course there are professional software that you can invest in. But if you want to start out you don't need much money. The production process has become less expensive. The development in recent years has not only brought up a higher

performance quality on desk top computers, but also prices have gone down.

The production of colourful story books is also an important bi- product of the tale. These story books, with pictures, illustrations, drawings and diagrams, with accompanying questions to test learners' understanding can be produced at different levels of learning. For example, animal tales can be exploited at the nursery and primary level, legends at the junior secondary level while myth at the senior secondary and high school level. The insistence on colours at the basic and primary level lends credence to the role colours play in attracting and holding the attention of young learners. The production of animated cartoons with the aid of 3-D computer- based cartoon programmes will render the tales available for diffusion by TV production houses. This will introduce to viewers a set of comics based on Cameroonian culture and history. On the production of cartoons, Grimm asserts:

It is cheaper to produce cartoons today. If you start with a comic strip, the first thing is for you to combine your ideas, you think of the story through and then you go and scribble, then you make an animation sheet where you have small drawings and then once you are done with that, either you scan those images or you colour them on the computer. Then you do certain camera movements like the zoom-in or close-up or you build those images again on the computer, once you are done... But on the internet, you can find free software, which you don't have to pay for.

Most are test software which the company offers for a limited time. But within that time frame, let's say thirty days or two months, you can use that software without any regulations and which can be good for the kind of project you are carrying out.

On this note he recommends the following computer programmes that can be used for cartoon production.

The popular ones are for pictures, and post-production photo shop. For editing it will either be I-movie on a max or on a PC it will be Movie-maker. These are already installed on those machines. But if you want to go in for more quality, you will go to Toon Boom Studio 4 on a max and to Adobe Premier on a PC. Those are the key tools that we work with.

From the above discussions and practical demonstrations and proposals geared towards redynamising the oral tale in an era of globalization, guided by the theory and practice of adaptation, Semiotics and New historicism, we have been able to render oral tale production relevant as a tool of entertainment, education, preservation and propagation of the cultural and historical values of any society through stage performances, movies and cartoons. With the aid of the internet, television and radio, we are sure to export the Cameroonian oral tale for example, to other parts of the world.

Bibliography

ABIOLA, Irele, 2001, *The African Experience: Literature in Africa and the Black Diaspora*, Oxford, Oxford University Press.

ADEJUNO,Arinpe,2009,*TechnologizingOralTexts:Archiving Yoruba Oral Literature through New Technological Media*, in LUMINA, Vol 20, No.2, Holy Name University, (1-16).www.researchgate.net/…/49601024/_technologizing_ oral texts_archiving…15/6/2014.

AKINDELE S.T., T.O. Gidado and D.R. Oloapo, 2002, *Globalisation, Its Implications and Consequences for Africa. In African Postcolonial Literature in English in the PostcolonialWeb.*www.postcolonialweb.org/africa/ akindele1b.html,26/02/2011.

ALBERTIS Window, *Analysis of Images-Words and Pictures.* www.newcastle-edu.au/discipline/fine-art/theory/analysis/an-words.htm.25/02/2011.

ALEMBONG, Nol, 1988, "Traditional Theatre among the Nweh of Cameroon", in *Theatre Camerounaise: Cameroon Theatre,* Eds. Bole Butake and Gilbert Doho, Yaounde, Bet and Co (Pub) Ltd.pp. 46 - 51.

----, 2010, Cameroon's Western Grassland Incantations: Background, Society, Cosmalogy, Cuvillier Verlag Gottingen.

----, 2011, *Standpoints on African Orature,* Yaounde, Presses Universitaires de Yaounde.

----, 2012, "A Case for a Dialogue of Cultures in the Era of Globalization", *Journal of English Language, Literature and Culture.Vol.1, No.1.,* pp. 31 - 44.

ANYIDOHO, Kofi et al., 1983, *Cross Rhythms: Papers in African Folklore.* Bloomington, Indiana: Trickster Press.

----, 1985, "The Present State of African Oral Literature Studies", *African Literature Studies: The Present State*

/ L'Etat Present, Ed. Stephen Arnold, Alberta, Three Continents Press and the Institute for Research in Comparative Literature, pp. 151 – 161.

----, 1983, "Scholarship and Vision: An Introduction" in *Cross Rhythms: Papers in African Folklore.* eds. Kofi Anyidoho et al. Bloomington, Trickster Press, pp.1 – 13.

ARTAUD, Antonin, 1998, "An End to Masterpieces (1933)", *Modern Theories of Drama: A Selection of Writings on Drama and Theatre 1850 – 1990.* Ed. George W. Brandt, Oxford, Clarendon Press, pp. 195 – 199.

ARIJON, Daniel, 1976, *Grammar of the Film,* Los Angeles, Silman-James Press.

ASTON, Elaine and George Savona, 1991, *Theatre as Sign-System: A Semiotics of Text and Performance,* London and New York, Routledge.

AUSLANDER, Philip, 2008, "Live and Technologically Mediated Performance," The *Cambridge Companion* to *Performance Studies*, Ed.Tracy C. Davis, Cambridge, Cambridge University Press. pp. 107 – 119.

BAKER-SMITH, Dominic, 2002, "Literature and the Visual Arts", *Encyclopedia of Literature and Criticism*, eds. Martin Coyle, Peter Garside, Malcolm Kelsall, and John Peck, New York and London, Routeledge. pp. 991 – 1003.

BALDICK, Chris, 2001, *Oxford Concise Dictionnary of Literary Terms*, Oxford: OUP.

BANKS, R.A., 1991, *Drama and Theatre Arts*, London, Hodder and Stoughton Educational.

BARNHILL, David Landis, Spring 2010, "Surveying the Landscape: A New Approach to Nature Writing", *Interdisciplinary Studies in Literature and Environment*, Ed. Scott Slovic, Volume 17, Issue 2. pp. 273 - 290.

BARTHES, Roland, 1985, "Rhetoric of the Image", *Semiotics: An Introductory Anthology*, Ed. Robert Innis, Bloomington, Indiana University Press. pp. 192 – 205.

BARTHES, Roland, 1963, *Elements of Semiology*, Hill and Wang, Meyer Schapiro.

BARTHES, Roland, 1977, *Rhetoric of the Image,*www. web.nmsu.edu/~jasheppe/courses/eng478_fall09/ barthes_rhethoric_image.pdf.

BASCOM, Williams, 1965, The Forms of Folklore: Prose, in The Journal of American Folklore, Vol.78, No 307,pp.3-20, www.ucs.louisiana.edu/ 5766/share/ BascomL1965.pdf, 12/8/2014.

BERKOWITZ, Doriet, 2011, *Oral Story telling: Building Community through Dialogue, Engagement, and Problem Solving by* The National Association for the Education of Young Children (36-40) *www://www. naeyc. org/tyc/files/tyc/file/V5I2/Oral%20Storytelling. pdf*

BERNETT, Michael, 2003, "From Wide Open Spaces to Metropolitan Places: The Urban Challenge to Ecocriticism", Eds. Michael P. Branch and Scott Slovic, Georgia, University of Georgia Press, pp. 296 - 318.

BIKOI, Charles Binam, 1985, "The Literary Dimension of Cameroon Cultural Identity", *The Cultural Identity of Cameroon*, Yaounde, Ministry of Information and Culture, Department of Cultural Affairs, pp. 89 – 99.

BINNS, Nial, 2003, "Landscapes of Hope and Destruction: Ecological Poetry in Spanish America", Eds. Michael P. Branch and Scott Slovic, Georgia, University of Georgia Press, pp. 124 -143.

BODUNDE, Charles A, 1992, "Oral Traditions and Modern Poetry: Okot P'Bitek's Song of Lawino and Okigbo's Labyrinths", *Orature in African Literature Today* (18), pp. 24 - 35.

BRADY, Ben, and Lance Lee, 1988, The Understructure of Writing for Film and Television, Austin, University of Texas Press.

BOJE, David M, 1998, The Post-modern Turn From Stories-as-Objects to Stories-in-Context Methods, in Academy of Management, Research Methods. www.cbae.nmsu.edu/~ dboje/measures.html, 26/02/2011.

BUCHAN, David, 2002, "Folk Literature", *Encyclopedia of Literature and Criticism,* Eds. Martin Coyle, Peter Garside, Malcolm Kelsall, and John Peck, New York and London, Routeledge. pp. 976 – 989.

BRUNEL, Adrian, 1948, *Film Script: The Technique of Writing for the Screen,* London, Burke Publishing Co.

BUTAKE, Bole and Guilbert Doho, Eds. 1988, Theatre Camerounais/Cameroonian Theatre, Proceedings of the Symposium on Cameroon Dramaturgy and Theatre Arts, Centre Camerounais de l"IIT.Bet and Co (Pub) Ltd.

BURKE, Carolyn L. and Joby G. Copenhauer, 2004, *Animal as People in Children's Literature, in Language Arts*, Vol. 81, No. 3, 2004. www.ncte.org/library/nctefiles/store/samplefiles/journals/la/la0813animals.pdf.10/2/2014.

CALABRESE, Omar. "Can Comics be Art? The Art of Comics, *ARTOON*", Ed. Electra Napoli, Rome, Elemond Editori Associati. pp. 35 – 37.

CAMPBELL, Jane. *Myths and Legends*, www.blake.com.cu/v/v spfliles/downloadables/iu22-myths-legends.pdf,11/2/2014.

CHAM, Mbye Baboucar, 1990, "Structural and Thematic Parallels in Oral Narrative and Film: Mandabi and Two African Oral Narratives", *The Oral Performance in Africa*, Ed. Isidore Okpewho, Ibadan: Spectrum Books Ltd, pp. 251–269.

CHILALA, Cheela and Jeremy Turner, 2005, *Adapting Literature into theatre: International Thoughts.* Notes

on a Forum held during the XVTH ASSITEJ Congress and General Assembly in Montreal, September 2005,www. aradgoch.org/documents/ADAPTING_LITERATURE_ INTO_THEATRE_%E2%80%93_INTERNATIONAL.

THOUGHTS_notes_of_a_seminar_held_in_the_ Montreal_ ASSITEL_Congress.pdf. 2/2/2014.

CRIMMENS, Paula, 2006, *Drama Therapy and Storymaking in Special Education*. London and Philadelphia, Jessica Kingsley Publishers.

CURTIS, Neal, 2009, "As If: Situating the Pictorial Turn", *Culture, Theory and Critique*, Ed. Neal Curtis Vol. 50, Issue 2 -3, pp. 95 – 101.

CULLER, Jonathan, 2001, *The Pursuit of Signs: Semiotics, Literature, Deconstruction,* London and New York, Routeledge.

DAVIES, Gill, 2000, *Create Your Own Stage Production.*

London, A & C Black (Publishers) Limited.

DICKINSON, Hugh, 1969, *Myth on the Modern Stage,* Urbana, University of Illonois Press.

DION, Birago, 1966, *Tales of Amadou Koumba*. Translated by Dorothy S. Blair, London, Oxford University Press.

DIOP, Birago, 1966, Tales of Amadou Koumba. London, Oxford University Press.

DINO, Felluga, *General Introduction to New Historicism.* www.sla.purdue.edu/academic/engl/theory/newhis toricism/modules/introduction.html.24/3/2012.

DORSON, Richard M,1963, Current Folklore Theories. In Current Anthropology. Vol. 4, No 1.1. (93-112) www.faculty.ksu.edu.sa/hujailan/trans/Current%20 Folklore%20Theories.doc. 12/5/2014.

DOYLE, Clar, 1993, "Raising Curtains on Education: Drama as a Site for Critical Pedagogy", *Critical Studies in Education and Cultural studies*, Eds. Henry A. Giroux and Paulo Freire, Westport, Greenwood Publishing Group, Inc.

DUNDES, Alan (Ed), 1965, *The study of Folklore*, London and New Jersey, Prentice-Hall, Inc.

EASTHOPE, Antony, 1991, *Literary into Cultural Studies*, London and New York, Routledge, 1991.

EBONG, Balbina, 2004,*The Use of Indigenous Techniques of Communication in Language Learning. The Case of Cameroon.* Ph.D Thesis, www.itsc.ph-karisruhe.de/ Ebong-Indegenoustechniques.pdf. 10/11/2013.

ECO, Umberto, 1998, "Semiotics of Theatrical Performance (1977)", *Modern Theories of Drama: A Selection of Writings on Drama and Theatre 1850 – 1990*, Ed. George W. Brandt, Oxford, Clarendon Press.

EJEDEPANG-KOGE, S.N. 1986, *The Tradition of a People*, Yaounde, SOPECAM.

----, S.N. 2001, "Culture" in *Know Yourself: Introducing Bakossiland. Lectures Delivered During The Tenth Anniversary Celebrations of TACUDA,* Ed. S.N. Ejedepang- Koge, Yaounde, SNEK Productions, pp. 178 – 181.

EISNER, Elliot W., 1972, *Educating Artistic Vision,* New York and London, Macmillan Publishing Co. Inc and Collier Macmillan Publishers.

EISNER, Will, 1996, *Graphic Storytelling and Visual Narrative: Principles and Practices from the Legendary Cartoonist,* New York, London, WW Norton and Company.

EKINDE-SONE, Bernard, Ivo, 2001, "Storytelling in Bakossiland", Know *Yourself: Introducing Bakossiland. Lectures Delivered During The Tenth Anniversary Celebrations of TACUDA,* Ed. S.N. Ejedepang-Koge, Yaounde, SNEK Productions, 2001: pp.187 – 193.

ELAINE, Aston and George Savona, 1991, *Theatre as Sign-System: A Semiotics of Text and Performance,* Routledge, New York.

ENOH, Ayang Frederick, 2012, *Green Hills: A Play on Environmental Protection*, Limbe, Presprint PLC.

ESSLIN, Martin, 1998, "The Signs of Stage and Screen (1987)", *Modern Theories of Drama: A Selection of Writings on Drama and Theatre 1850 – 1990.* Ed. George W. Brandt, Oxford, Clarendon Press.

ESTOK, Simon, 2009, "Theorizing in a Space of Ambivalent Openness: Ecocriticism and Ecophobia", *Interdisciplinary Studies in Literature and Environment*, Ed. Scott Slovic, Volume 16, 2, pp. 203 - 225.

ETHERTON, Michael, 1979, "Trends in African Theatre", *African Literature Today: Retrospect and Prospect*, Ed. Eldred Durosimi Jones, London, pp. 57 – 86.

ETTIN, Andrew V.ed., 1984, *Literature and the Pastoral*, New Haven and London, Yale University Press.

EYOH, Ndumbe,1986, *Hammocks to Bridges: Report on the Workshop on Theatre for Integrated Rural Development, Kumba, Cameroon,1-16 December,1984*, Yaounde, BET.

FINE, Elizabeth C, 1984, *The Folktale Text: From Performance to Print*, Bloomington, Indiana University Press.

FINNEGAN, Ruth, 1970, *Oral Literature in Africa*, Nairobi, Oxford University Press.

GINKEL, Hans, 2000, *Roundtable Dialogue among Civilizations, UNESCO celebrates the United Nations Year of Dialogue among Civilisations,* www.unesco.org/dialogue/en/ginkel.htm.12/5/2014.

-----, 2006, *Point of View/Hans Van Ginkel: Yokohama Conference to focus on Cooperation,* Herald International Tribune, The New York Times, www.archive.unu.edu/globalization/2006/files/Ginkel_Asahi_POV.pdf ,12/5/2014.

GIROUX, Henry, 2001, *Breaking into the Movies: Pedagogy and the Politics of Film*, www.jaconlinejournal.com/ archives/vol 21.3/giroux-breaking.pdf, 20/5/2014.

FOMINYEN, Pani Nalova Marianne, 2008, "Production of Docudrama on Widowhood Rights: The Case of Bali Nyonga", Masters Dissertation, University of Yaounde I.

FONLON, Bernard, 1982, "Idea of Literature", *Abbia: Cameroon Cultural Review*, Ed. Bernard Fonlorn, Yaounde: CEPER, pp. 175 - 212.

FROUG, William, 1972, *The Screenwriter Looks at the Screenwriter*, New York, Dell Publishing Co, Inc.

FURNISS, Grahan and Liz Gunner, 1995, "Introduction: Power, Marginality and Oral Literature", *Power, Marginality and African Oral Literature*, Eds. Graham Furness and Liz Gunner, Cambridge, Cambridge University Press. pp. 1 – 19.

GALLI, Silvano, 1983, "Storytelling Among the Anyi-Bona", *Cross Rhythms*: *Papers in African Folklore*, Eds. Kofi Anyidoho, Daniel Avorgbedor, Susan Domowitz and Eren Grey-Saul, Bloomington, Trickster Press. pp. 13 - 42.

GESKELL, Ronald, 1972, *Drama and Reality: the European Theatre since Ibsen*. London, Routledge and Kegan Paul.

GILLES, Breton and Michel Lambert, 2003, *Globalisation et Universités: Nouvel Espace, Nouveau Acteurs*, Québec, Canada, Les presses de l'Université Laval / Economica.

GOLDSTEIN, kenneth, 1964, *A Guide for Field Workers in Folklore,* Hatboro, Pensylvania, Folklore Associates, Inc.

GROTOWASKI, Jerzy, 1998, "The Theatre's New Testament (1964), *Modern Theories of Drama: A Selection of Writings on Drama and Theatre 1850 – 1990,* Ed. George W. Brandt , Oxford, Clarendon Press.

GUNERATNE, Anthony R., 2004, "Introduction: Rethinking Third Cinema," *Rethinking Thirrd Cinema*, Eds. Anthony

R. Guneratne and W.D., New York and London, Routledge, Taylor and Francis Group. pp. 1 – 25.

HADAD, Ivan and Hiten Patel, Cultural Influences in Japanese and AmericanAnimation,www.honors.uiuc. edu/ealc15097/HitenIvan/culture.htm,2/3/2011

HEDGES, Warren, New Historicism Explained www.sou. edu/English/Hedges/Sodashop.Rcenter/Theory/ Explained/nhistexp.html.10/2/2000.

HARRIS, Mike, 2007, "Introduction to Script writing" *The Handbook of Creative Writing*, Ed. Steven Earnshaw, Edingburg, Edinburg University Press, pp. 251 - 262.

HONZI, Jindrich, 1998, "Dynamics of the Sign in the Theatre (1940)", *Modern Theories of Drama: A Selection of Writings on Drama and Theatre 1850 – 1990,* Ed. George W. Brandt, Oxford, Clarendon Press.

HUTCHEON, Linda, *From Page to Stage to Screen: The Age of Adaptation*.www.canadianshakespeares.ca/essays/ hutcheon-page-stage.pdf, 4/6/2014.

INNIS, Robert E., 1985, Ed. "Introduction" *Semiotics: An Introductory Anthology*. Bloomington, Indiana University Press, pp. vii - xvi.

IYASERE, Solomon O., 1980, "African Oral Tradition-Criticism as a Performance: A Ritual" *African Literature Today,* Vol. 11. Ed. pp. 168 – 174.

JASON, Heda, 1977, "A Model for Narrative Structure in Oral Literature", Patterns *in Oral Litarature*, Eds. Heda Jason and Dimitri Segal, The Hague and Paris, Mouton Publishers, 1977. pp. 99 – 139.

KAES, Anton, 1995, "Media and Nations: Global Communication and Cultural Identity", *Cultural Dialogue and Misreading*, Eds. Mabel Lee and Meng Hua, University of Sydney World Literature, Series No. 1 Sydney, Wild Peony Pty Ltd. pp. 299 – 303.

KERN, Robert, 2009, "Birds of a Feather: Emily Dickson, Alberto Manguel and the Nature Poet's Dilemma, *Interdisciplinary Studies in Literature and Environment*, Ed. Scott Slovic, Volume 16, 2, pp. 327 - 343.

KERR, David, 1995, *African Popular Theatre: From Pre-colonial Times to the Present Day,* London, James Curry Ltd.

KLAPPROTH, Daniele, 2007, "Narrating across Cultural Boundaries – Or Where were Rocky's Father's

Brothers?", Cultures *in Contact*, Eds. Balz Engler and Lucia Michalcak, Zurich, SAUTE. pp. 77 – 93.

KNAPPERT, Jan, 1971, "Myths and Legends of the Congo". Nairobi, London, Ibadan: Heinemann Educational Books, 1971.

LEE, Lance and Ben Brady, 1988, *The Understructure of Writing for Film and Television*, Austin, University of Texas Press.

LOVEJOY, Margot, 2004, *Digital Currents: Art in the Electronic Age*. New York and London, Routledge, 2004.

LUPOFF, Dick and Don Thompson, 1973 "Introduction", *The Comic-Book Book*. Eds. Don Thompson and Dick Lupoff, U.S.A., Library of Congress Cataloging in Publication Data. pp.1– 7.

LYONS, M.C., 1995, *The Arabian Epic: Heroic and Oral Story-telling*. Vol 1, Cambridge, Cambridge University Press.

MACKAY, Wand J.,1948, *Film Script*. London, Burke Publishing Co.

MARSCHALL, Richard, 1997, *America's Great Comic Strips Artists: From the Yellow Kid to Peanuts*, New York, Boundtable Press.

MEHRING, Margaret, 1990, *The Screenplay: A Blend of Film Form and Content*, Boston, London, Focal Press.

MIEDER, Wolfgang , 1987, *Tradition and Innovation in Folk Literature*, Hanover and London, University Press of New England.

MOUNIN, George, 1985, *Semiotic Praxis: Studies in Pertinence and in the Means of Expression and Communication*, New York, Plenum Press.

GRUMBIN, Edward, 1999, "Going to Basho's Pine: Wilderness Education for the Twenty-First Century", in ISLE, vol 6(2), p.121-133.

HARROW, Kenneth W., 1994, *Thresholds of Change in African Literature: The Emergence of a Tradition*, Portsmouth and London, Heinemann and James Currey.

KIESLERS, Frederick, 1982, "Endless Innovations" In *Theory and Science Design*, ed. R.L. Held, Ann Arbor, Michigan, UMI Research Press.

LELLIS, George, 1982, Bertolt Brecht: Cahier du Cinéma and Contemporary Film Theory, Ann Arbor, Michigan, UMI Research Press.

LANDY, Robert, 1982, *Handbook of Educational Drama and Theatre,* Westport, Connecticut.

POLLOCK, Dela, 2005, Remembering: Oral History as Performance, Palgrave, Macmillan.

PORTNOY, Kenneth, 1991, *Screen Adaptation. A Scriptwriting Handbook*, Stoneham, Focal Press.

MACKAY, W, J. 1948, *Film Script*, London, Burke Publishing Co.

MADIYA, Clémentine Fai Nzuji, 1985, "Modes de Transmission, de Circulation et de Conservation de

Oeuvres Orales", *Oral Literature in Africa Today: Theoretical and Practical Approaches, Eds. Louis-Marie Ongoum and Isaac-Célestin Tcheho*, pp. 25 – 38.

MATSUURA, Koichiro, 2005, "Globalization, Intangible Cultural Heritage and the Role of UNESCO", *Globalization and Intangible Cultural Heritage,* Ed. Laura Wong, Tokyo, Japan, UNESCO and United Nations University, 2005.

MARIN–ARRESE, Juana I., 2006, *Cognition and Culture in Political Cartoons*, University of Dursburg – Essen, LAUD University Agency.

MBANGWANA, Paul Nkad, 1983, "Cameroon Tales in Ngemba: A Study in Language and Social Setting." Doctorat D'Etat Thesis, University of Yaounde I.

MEIDER, Wolfgang, 1987, *Tradition and Innovation in Folk Literature*, Hanover and London, University Press of New England.

MEDUBI, Oyinkan, 2002, *Language and Ideology in Nigerian Cartoons*, University of Duisburg-Essen, LAUD linguistic Agency.

MEHRING, Margaret, 1990, The Screenplay: A Blend of Film Form and Content, Boston and London, Focal Press.

McCLOUD, Scott, 1993, *Understanding Comics: The Invisible Art.* New York. Harper Collins Publishers, Inc.

MACGOWAN, Kenneth, 1965, *Behind the Screen: The History and Techniques of the Motion Picture,* New York, A Delacorte Press Book.

MBUNWE-SAMBA, Patrick, 1989, "Oral Literature and Education," *Oral Literature in Africa Today: Theoretical and Practical Approaches,* Eds. Louis-Marie Ongoum and Isaac-Célestin Tcheho, pp. 89 - 97.

MERREL, Floyd, 2001, "Charles Sanders Peire's Concept of the Sign", The Routeledge Companion to Semiotics and Linguistics, Ed. Paul Cobley, London and New York, Routeledge. pp. 43 - 52.

MILLER, William, 1980, *Screenwriting for Narrative Film and Television*, London, Columbus Books.

MITTELL, Jason, 2007, "Film and Television Narrative, *The Cambridge Companion to Narrative,* Ed. David Herman, Cambridge, Cambridge University Press. pp. 156 – 171.

MONTFORT, Nick, 2007, "Narrative and Digital Media", *The Cambridge Companion to Narrative,* Ed. David Herman, Cambridge, Cambridge University Press. pp. 172 – 185.

MORSE, Richard, 2009, *Theatre: Its Healing Role in Education*. New York, Vantage Press, 2009.

MPHANDE, Lupenga, 2003, "Oral Literature and Performance", *Encyclopedia of African Literature*, Ed. Simon Gikandi, London and New York, Routledge, Taylor and Francis Group. pp. 406 – 421.

NGOME, Victor Epie, 1992, *What God has put Asunder*, Yaounde, Pitcher Books Ltd.

NGUMU, Pie-Claude, 1985, "General Introduction To The Colloquium Theme and Methodology", *The Cultural*

Identity of Cameroon, Yaounde, Ministry of Information and Culture, Department of Cultural Affairs, pp. 19 - 22.

NJOYA, Adamu Ndam, 1985, "Cultural Identity and Cooperation between Nations", *The Cultural Identity of Cameroon,* Yaounde, Department of Cultural Affairs, Ministry of Information and Culture, pp. 143 - 157.

NKWI, Paul Nchoji, 1989, *The German Presence in the Western Grassfields, 1891-1913: A German Colonial Account*, Research Report No.37, The Netherlands, African Studies Centre Leiden,www.openaccess.leidenuniv.nl/bitstream/--/ASC-1236144-111.pdf.

NOËL, Carroll, 1996, *Theorizing the Moving Image*, Cambridge, Cambridge University Press.

NORRICK, Neal R., 2007, "Conversational Storytelling", *The Cambridge Companion to Narrative,* Ed. David Herman, Cambridge, Cambridge University Press. pp. 127 – 139.

OGUNDELE, Wole, 1992, "Orality Versus Literacy in Mazisi Kunene's Emperor Shaka the Great", *African Literature Today*, pp. 1- 9.

OJOADE. J. Olowo, 1989, "African Moral Education Seen Through Oral Literature Together with Foreign Analogues" *Oral Literature in Africa Today: Theoretical and Practical Approaches,* Eds. Louis-Marie Ongoum and Isaac-Célestin Tcheho: pp. 99 – 118.

OKAFOR, Clement, 2004, *Oral Tradition and Civic Education in Africa*, International Education Journal

Vol 5, No 3, www.files.eric.ed.gov/fulltext/E1903865. pdf.23/5/2014.

OKPEWHO, Isidore, Ed. 1980, "Rethinking Myth", African *Literature Today,* No. 11. pp. 5 – 24.

----, 1988, "The Modern Writer and the Oral Tradition."in *African Literature Today* No.16. pp. 1- 25.

----, 1990, "The Study of Performance", *The Oral Performance in Africa*, pp. 1-21.

OKECHUKWU, Mezu, Ed. 1971, *Modern Black Literature*, Buffalo, New York Bllack Pcademy Press, Inc.

OKPEWHO, Isidore, Ed. 1990, *The Oral Performance in Africa,* Ibadan, Spectrum Books Limited.

----, 1992, *African Oral Literature: Backgrounds, Character and Continuity,* Idiana, Indiana University Press.

----, 1979, *The Epic in Africa: Toward a Poetics of the Oral Performance,* New York, Columbia University Press, 1979.

OLIVA, Achille Bonito, 1989, "Artoonia", *Artoon*, Ed. Electra Napoli, Rome, Elemond Editori Associati. 1989. pp. 15 – 21.

OMOTOSO, Kole, "Concepts of History and Theatre", *A History of Theatre in Africa,* Ed. Martin Banham, Cambridge, Cambridge University Press. pp. 1 -12.

OWUOR, Jenipher, 2007, "Integrating African Indigenous knowledge in Kenya's Formal Education system: The

Potential for sustainable Development". In *Journal of Contemporary Issues in Education*, 2 (2) pp 21-37 www.ejournals.library.ualberta.ca/index.php/JCIE, 20/8/2014.

PAVIS, Patrice, 1976, *Probleme de Sémiologie Théâtrale*, Quebec, Presse de l'Université du Quebec.

PEIRCE, Charles S., 1985, "Logic as Semiotic. The Theory of Signs", *Semiotics: An Introductory Anthology*. Ed. Robert Innis, Bloomington, Indiana University Press. pp. 4 – 23.

PEPICELLO, W.J. and Thomas A Green, 1984, *The Language of Riddles: New Perspectives.* Columbus, Ohio State University Press.

PEARSALL, Judy et al. ed. 2003, *Oxford Dictionary of English*. Oxford: Oxford University Press.

PELICAN, Michael, 2006, *Getting along in the Grass fields: Interethnic Relations and Identity Politics in Northwest Cameroon,* P.hD Thesis. Martin-Luther-Universitat Halle-Wittenberg, www.michaelapelican.com/pelican-publications presentations.pdf, 10-3-2004.

PETRICCA, Stefano, 1989, "Artoonist", *ARTOON*, Ed. Electra Napoli, Rome, Elemond Editori Associati. pp. 23 – 33.

PETERSON, Mike and Jennifer Hind, 2005, *Folk Tales and Fables: Curriculum Guide*. 2014,www.weeklystorybook. com/files/folktalesguide.pdf, 1-52. 6/10/2014.

PORTNOY, Kenneth, 1991, *Screen Adaptation: A Scriptwriting Handbook*, Stoneham, Focal Press.

PRICE, Lindsay, 2004, *Adapting a Play*, www.theatrefolk. com/freebies/adapting-a-play.pdf, 20/3/2012.

RAINER, John, 2005, And Martin Lewis, *Teaching Drama and Theatre in the Secondary school*, Abingdon, Routledge, www.Samples.sainsburysebooks.co.uk/9781134 365234_Sample_534745.pdf,25/02/2013

RICHARDSON, Brian, 2007, "Drama and Narrative", *The Cambridge Companion to Narrative,* Ed. David Herman, Cambridge, Cambridge University Press.

RIDOUT, Nicholas, 2008, "Performance and Democracy", *The Cambridge Companion to Performance Studies*, Ed. Tracy C. Davis, Cambridge. Cambridge University Press. pp. 11 – 21.

RILLA, Wolf, 1974, *The Writer and the Screen: On Writing for Film and Television*, New York, William Morrow and Company Inc.

ROBERT Con Davis and Ronald Schleifer, 1989, *Contemporary Literary Criticism: Literary and Cultural Studies*, New York and London, Longman Inc., 1989.

ROSENBERG, Donna, 1997, *Folklore, Myths and Legends : A World Perspective*, Illinois, NTC Publishing Group.

ROSS, Malcolm, 1982, *The Development of Aesthetic Experience*, Pergamon Press.

RYAN, Marie-Laure, 2007, "Toward a Definition of narrative", *The Cambridge Companion to Narrative,* Ed. David Herman, Cambridge, Cambridge University Press. pp. 22 – 33.

SCHAPIRO, Meyer, 1985, "On Some Problems in the Semiotics of Visual Art: Field and Vehicle in Image-Signs", *Semiotics: An Introductory Anthology*. Ed. Robert Innis, Bloomington, Indiana University Press. pp. 206 – 271.

SCHIPPER, Mineke, 1977, "Oral tradition and African theatre" (123-134), In Mineke Schipper-de leeuw (ed) *African Perspectives Text and context: Methodological explorations in the field of African Literature*, 1977/1, www//openaccess.leidenuniv.nl/bitstream/handle/.../ 05_090_065.pdf?...1 20/5/2014.

SCHOLES Robert and Robert Kellogg, 1966, *The Nature of Narrative,* London, Oxford University Press.

SCHOLES, Robert, 1983, *Semiotics and Interpretation,* Yale, Yale University Press.

SCHMID, Herta and Aloysius Van Kesteren. Eds., 1984, New Perspectives in the Theory of Drama and Theatre; an Introduction, in *Semiotics of Drama and Theatre: New Perspectives in the Theory of Drama and Theatre,* Amsterdam, Philadelphia, John Benjamins Publishing Company.

SEGERS, Rien T., 1995, "Cultural Identity: New Perspective for Literary Studies" *Cultural Dialogue and Misreading,* Eds. Mabel Lee and Meng Hua University of Sydney World Literature Series, 1. Sydney, Wild Peony Pty Ltd. pp. 313 – 327.

SEITEL, Peter, 1998, *See So that We May See: Performaces and Interpretations of Traditional Tales from Tanzania*, Bloomington and London.

SIMMS, Laura, *Thinking Like a Storyteller: The Living Context.*

www.laurasimms.com/essaycontext.html.25/04/2012.

STAM, Robert, 2005, "Introduction: The Theory and Practice of Adaptation", *Literature and Film: A Guide to the Theory and Practice of Film Adaptation*, Eds. Robert Stam and Alessandra Raengo, Malden, Blackwell Publishing Ltd.

STAM, Robert, 2008, "Introduction: The Theory and Practice of Adaptation", *Literature and Film: A Guide to the Theory and Practice of Film Adaptation*, Eds. Robert Stam and Alessandra Raengo, Carlton, Victoria, Blakwell Publishing. pp. 1 – 47

STRACZYNSKI, J. Michael, 1982,*The Complete Book of Script Writing,* Cincinnati, Ohio Writer's Digest Books.

STRATTON, Florence, 1994, *Contemporary African Literature and the Politics of Gender*, London and New York, Routledge, 1994.

STYAN, J.L., 1969, *The Elements of Drama*, Cambridge, Cambridge University Press.

SWAIN, Dwight Vand Joye R.Swain, 1988, *Film Scriptwriting: A Practical Manual*, Boston, London, Focal Press.

TAIWO, Oladele. 1967, *An Introduction to West African Literature,* London, Thomas Nelson and Sons Ltd, 1967.

TALA, Kashim I., 1989, *The Oral Tale in Africa*, Yaounde, BET and Co (Pub) Ltd.

----, 1999, *Orature in Africa,* Saskatchewan, University of Saskatchewan Press.

----, 2012, "Kashimism: Representing Voices", Journal *of English Language, Literature and Culture, Vol.1, Num. 1.* pp. 15 - 30.

----, 2013, *Cameroon Oral Literature: An Introduction,*

Kansas City, Miraclaire Academic Publications.

----, 2013, *Orature: A Research Guide,* Kansas City, Miraclaire Academic Publications.

TAPPING, Craig, 1990, *Voices off: Models of orality in Africa Literature and Literary criticism.* ARIEL: A Review of Intenrational English Literature, 21:3, July

1990 - (73-87) www.ariel.journalhosting.ucalgary.ca/ ariel/ index.php/ariel/article/..../2247, 25/05/2014.

TAUSSIG, Michael, July – Nov. 2009, "What Do Drawings Want?", *Culture, Theory and Critique*, Ed. Neal Curtis, Vol. 50, Issue 2 -3., pp. 263 – 274.

THOMPSON, Don and Dick Lupoff, 1973, "Introduction", *The Comic-Book Book*, Eds. Don Thompson and Dick Lupoff, USA, Library of Congress Cataloging in Publication Data. pp. 20 - 30.

THOMPSON, Stith, 1977, *The Folktale.* California, University of California Press.

TONKIN, Elizabeth, 1992, *Narrating Our Past: The Social Construction of Oral History*, Cambridge, Cambridge University Press.

TOM Fish and Jennifer Perkins, 2002, *Terms Used by New Historicism* www.sla.purdue.edu/academic/engl/theory/newhistoricism/terms/index.html, 15/05/2012.

TOOLAN, Michael, 2007, "Language", *The Cambridge Companion to Narrative,* Ed. David Herman, Cambridge, Cambridge University Press. pp. 231 – 243.

UKADIKE, N. Frank, 2004, "Video Booms and the Manifestations of "First" Cinema in 'Anglophone Africa", *Rethinking Third Cinema*, Eds. Anthony R. Guneratne and Wimal Dissanayake, New York and London, Routledge, Taylor and Francis Group. pp. 126–141.

UKALA, Sam, 1992, "Plot and Conflict in African Folktales", African Literature Today (18), pp. 62 - 73.

WACHUKU, Ukachi N. and Chisimdi Udoka Ihentuge, 2010, *The Nigeria Film Industry and Literacy Adaptation. The Journey of Things Fall Apart from Page to Screen,* www.ajol.info/index.php/cajtms/article/download/76563/67012, 12/8/2014.

WALLIS, Mick and Simon Shepherd, 2002, *Studying Plays*, London, Arnold Publishers.

WALTER, Richard, 1988, *Screenwriting: The Art, Craft and Business of Film and Television Writing.* New York, Penguin Books.

WANJALA, Chris, 2003, The Growth of a Literary Tradition in East Africa: An Inaugural Lecture delivered at the University of Nairobi.www.uonbi.ac.ke/sites/default/-files/wanjala.pdf.

WASTBERG, Per, 1988, "The Writer in Modern Africa", *Criticism and Ideology*, Ed. Kirsten Holst Petersen, Upsala, Scandinavian Institute of African Studies. pp. 45-62.

WAYNE, Don E. "New Historicism", *Literature and the Pastoral*, Ed. ETTIN, Andrew V., New Haven and London, Yale University Press. pp. 791 – 803.

WEE, Su Jeong, 2009, "A case study of Drama Education Curriculum for Young Children", *Early Children Programs Journal of Research in Childhood Education*, Vol 1, 23, No 4, pp. 1 - 17.

WINSTON, Joe, 1998, *Drama, Narrative and Moral Education: Exploring Traditional Tales in the Primary Years,* London, Washington D.C. UK Palmer Press.

WITHROW, Steven, 2003, *Toon Art: The Graphic Art of Digital Cartooning,* Michigan, Watson-Guptil Publications

WYVER, John, 1989, *The Moving Image: An International History of Film, Television and Video,* Oxford and London, Basil Blackwell Inc and British Film Institute.

Appendices

APPENDIX 1: Selected Tales under Adaptation:

Yomandene and the Stubborn Son

(Narrated by Hannah Efosi Luma in the presence of her two daughters and this researcher in Bokwango, Buea,2015.)

Hannah Efosi: *Maito kai!*

Children:

Hannah Efosi: *Boys and girls, I want to tell you a story!*

Children: *What is your story all about?*

Once upon a time, there was a man who had a wife and two sons. They were farmers. Whenever they went to the farm, they would clear a large portion of the forest for farming. But something strange always happened when they got up the following day. Whenever they visited the cleared portion of land, they would find out that it was all covered with trees and shrubs again. This continued for a long time and they were greatly troubled.

One day they decided to find out what mysterious force was behind the strange happening. In the night they went to the farmland and hid by a nearby shrub. Close to midnight, they heard a frightening and loud voice of a beast, accompanied by the following words:

Mauja, mauja, temeke jinja ! mauja, mauja, temeke jinja !

While the beast was shouting and approaching, the forest in front of it gave way and there was a clear path. When the boys saw it, they were terrified and rushed back home to report what they had seen to their father. Their father decided to help them fabricate two similar arrows that they would use to chase or kill the beast. They pleaded that their father accompany them to the forest the following day, but he refused. Since they were courageous, they decided to go and challenge the beast which was known throughout the surrounding villages as *Yomandene.*

When they got to the farm, they waited for the beast, but it did not come as expected. While they lay waiting, they fell asleep. At that moment, the beast started approaching with a loud sound. The younger son was woken by the following words uttered by the beast:

Mauja, mauja, temeke jinja !
mauja, mauja, temeke jinja !

He struggled to wake his elder brother up to no avail. In a state of fright, he mistakenly snatched his elder brother's arrow, aimed at the beast and shot it. The arrow hit the beast on its head and it groaned:

eeeeeeh, na wolio! eeeeeeh,
na wolio! meaning

I am dead oh!
I am dead oh!

In pains, it began retreating into its hiding place. The tremors produced by its huge body woke his elder brother, who was deep asleep, up. When he got up his younger brother blamed him for his sleeping attitude. He also reported how the beast made its way to the farmland, and how he tried in vain to wake him up but could not because he was fast asleep. At this juncture, the elder brother looked for his arrow and did not find it. When he asked about the whereabouts of his arrow, his younger brother, in fright, intimated that he mistakenly used it to shoot at the beast. Angered by this revelation, his elder brother exclaimed:

You have killed me!
You have killed me!

The younger brother pleaded with him to take his own arrow but to no avail. He insisted on having the same arrow his father gave him. He insisted until they got home. When they got home, the younger brother narrated the story to his parents. Their mother pleaded with his embittered son to no avail. Their father also pleaded with his elder son in vain. He insisted on having back the arrow that he left home with. He insisted on having his arrow claiming that it was more beautiful than that of his younger brother. The younger brother said that since his elder brother was insisting, he would go into the forest and look for the missing arrow. His mother handed him *kwakoko bible*, a local porridge made out of pounded cocoyams, and wished him success.

So, early the next morning he set out for the forest in search of the missing arrow. His long trek took him to *Yomandene's* village. The beast was known in that village as *munanga mo njo é titi*. On his way to the village where the beast lived, he met an old woman. She was a devil that lived in the forest. She had wounds all over her body that produced a nauseating odour. He was courageous to confront the woman. When she saw him she exclaimed:

I have got a son!

Then he replied:

I have got a mother!

The old woman had nothing to offer the boy as food. So, she gave him fowl dung to eat. When the boy tried to eat it, it turned into rice and he started eating. He spent the whole night in her hut. The next day she gave him kernel oil, popularly known as *manyanga,* to rub all over her body. He did not hesitate. He started applying it all over her body. So she blessed him saying:

As you move on my son, your path will be clear. Nothing will stand as obstacle to you. Your eyes will be clear to see well!

As he moved on, he met another hut covered with shrubs. In it lived another old woman. When he entered and saw her, he asked:

Why are you living in a hut covered with grass?

She replied:

I am alone my son and there is no one to help me.

So, he took a hatchet and began clearing the grass on the hut. She was happy and wondered aloud:

What a nice child!

He said he wished he could stay longer but he was on his way in search of his elder brother's arrow. The woman told him that she knew his destination and mission and warned that the person he intended to meet was too powerful and fiery to confront. She promised to give him powerful charms to confront the beast. She also informed him of the presence of a river which was very difficult to cross. She also said the man's name was *munanga mo njo é titi*. She instructed the boy saying:

> *When you get to the village don't reveal your mission to anyone. Also pretend you are missing. The children of Munanga mo Njo etiti will find you and take you to his house. Also look for two calabash pots. Pour water in one and palm wine in the other. You should also wail saying that you didn't know he had died. As you cry, break the calabash with water. When you will try to break the second calabash, they will restrain you. You will tell them that you are related to their father. This will make them welcome you in their midst. They will also take you around and show you the arrow that killed him.*

The old woman handed him *njombi* known as elephant stock, and said that he should immerse it in the river.

When he got to the river, he dipped the elephant stock into the river and a bridge appeared which he used to cross the river. When he crossed the river, he removed the stock and the bridge disappeared. When he got to the beast's village, he started crying and did what he had been instructed by the old woman. While he cried the people came out wondering aloud:

So, this wicked man had relatives?

So, they took him to the house where the beast lived. They showed him the beast's children and the arrow that killed him. The boy cried and went closer to the arrow saying:

So, this is the arrow that killed you? Who did this to you?

So, they begged and asked him to stop crying. They also showed him a room where he would spend the night. The home of the beast revealed its wealth including cattle and farms. He stayed in the beast's home for one week. During this time, he hunted animals and birds with the arrow that was used to kill *Yomandene*. Whenever he missed his target, he would exclaim:

Oh! this is how I missed munanga mo njo é titi.

He said this forgetting he was in the midst of the beast's children. When they heard this, the children exclaimed:

So, you are the one who killed our father?

When he realized his error, he joined them crying and also pleaded his innocence. His voice drowned those of the beast's children. When they got home, he complained to their mother that the children have made him remember the death of his uncle.

When he realized that his real identity would soon be discovered, he started planning how to steal the arrow and escape. One day he succeeded to deceive the beast's children to go ahead of him. When they left, he tarried behind and stole the arrow.

The other villagers were also jealous of the boy's presence and feared he had come to inherit the man's wealth. So they planned to kill him. There was a cock in the village that guarded the village against strangers and criminals. It also crowed when everybody had left. When he tried to escape, the cock crowed saying he was alone in the village. So, the villagers who heard the cock crowing rushed back to find out what had happened.

When they arrived the village, they found out that their stranger had escaped. So, they chased him. But when he got to the river, he used the elephant stock to cross the river as he did before. When he had crossed the river, he removed it again and the bridge disappeared. When his enemies got to the river, they were stranded. Those who knew how to swim jumped into the river and continued chasing him.

He ran until he got to the house of the old woman with wounds all over her body. He hid himself there. When the people entered the house the odour from the old woman's wounds made them run out of the house. So, they gave up the chase and went back. The old woman gave him an egg and said this was where her wealth has been stored saying:

when you get home, look for an open space, clear it and break the egg on the cleared spot. Then you will see what will come out of it.

When he got home, he handed his elder brother's spear to him. Then he cleared an open area and broke the egg. A beautiful mansion appeared on the space. When his brother saw it, he became jealous of his younger brother. So, he decided that he must also get rich. The younger brother was also given a bird by the witch. The bird could sing well and it had a lovely voice that attracted many onlookers. After listening to the bird, they would give the owner money and even material things. So, the younger brother grew richer and richer.

One day he left for the farm. In his absence, his elder brother took the bird to make some money for himself. When he threw up the bird, it flew away. When the younger brother arrived, and asked about the whereabouts of his singing bird his elder said that the bird flew away far to the forest. His younger brother insisted to have back his bird. So, in pride, he left in search of the bird.

On his way he found two animals fighting. Instead of separating them, he killed one of them. As he moved further, he met two people fighting. Instead of separating them and bringing peace, he joined in the fighting.

When he came across the woman with wounds, he mocked at her wounds and refused to eat what was given him. So, the old woman cursed him saying:

You will never see good, and your path will be thorny!

He did not care to apologize but proudly left her presence and went away.

When he met the old woman living in the house covered with shrubs, he mocked her for living in a hut infested with lice. The old woman also got angry and cursed him. When he got to the beast's village he was arrested, charged with stealing the arrow and killed. The singing bird returned to the village and there was feasting and celebration.

APPENDIX 2: Interviews

Interview with Fon Angwafor of Mankon in his Mankon Palace on 10 January 2010.

Taku Victor: Your Highness! What do you blame for the gradual disappearance of the storytelling event in Cameroon?

Fon Angwafor III: The society is fast changing to the detriment of this nation, Cameroon. We are speaking English and not our local languages. Do not forget that language is an important element of a culture. So by adopting English, Cameroonians have become foreigners in their homeland. The customs and traditions of the colonial masters seem to be gaining grounds than the authentic culture and traditions of Cameroonians. The system of education being practiced in Cameroon is foreign. Storytelling used to be an important aspect of education. The children were educated by their own teachers through storytelling while the teachers served as parents. While the children listened to these tales, they were anxious and inquisitive. Today, there is a dramatic change. All the attention of children and parents is on the television, which is also foreign. Those who operate these TV stations are foreign. They have been taught and trained by foreigners. They have also been trained to execute and appreciate what the makers of the television want. Do not forget that the television and radio are used to denigrate the culture of Cameroon. The exercise of crowning and honouring those who have achieved something with a feather as a mark of recognition is today considered primitive. In the days past, it was a source of inspiration to hunters and warriors to lure them towards success. Even journalists over the radio and television question the raison d'être of the red feather. They even laugh at the habit of eating the gizzard by elders. Every aspect of Cameroon culture is being mocked by children trained by foreigners. Today, many talented citizens have been educated to transmit what they learnt in those foreign institutions to ignorant Cameroonians. Most of them have not been educated to carry out research in their home countries so that they can contribute to the development of their nation. Those who study in Europe prefer the foolish things they see there. I also blame all these on the kinds of textbooks being used in our schools. They are tailored to meet the needs of American and European thoughts. Today, a teacher has to be paid before teaching. He is even not satisfied with his little pay. They are more interested in more money and patriotism is not in them. Today, degrees, and not morality, are respected. Even teachers have been brought up to dispose of the African culture and tradition. If storytelling worked, it is because it had no rival. Unfortunately, much research has not been carried out on it. It is not on the syllabus and curriculum.

Book writers have not written valuable material on it. I fear that before long, we will neither be Africans, Europeans nor Americans. Your research on this is timely. I wish that those who are in charge of our education retrieve what is in our culture and document it. And those in charge of the up-bringing of the children make it possible that they be properly taught.

Taku Victor: Your Highness, can you trace when the telling of tales began dwindling in practice and importance?

Fon Angwafor III:

This was after independence. During this period, there was euphoria for Cameroonians to go abroad and study. Those who went there to study appreciated life and tradition in Europe and America. The get-rich- quick syndrome took over the minds of Cameroonians. Cameroon has a consumer population and not a productive one. Because of lack of patriotism, all our cocoa, coffee, cotton are refined out of Cameroon. And so we are producers of raw material and consumers of refined goods. The scholarships granted to Cameroonians to study abroad were intended to train people who would come and improve the Cameroonian situation. It was not meant for people to come and earn better salaries. But today, Cameroonians trained in industrialized countries are expected to fit well in an agricultural and developing country. Most of them go back in search of jobs in these industrialized countries. Cameroonians have grown to challenge what is original, authentic, natural and traditional. If we put the African side by side the European, we will see the need to preserve the important values of their culture. The white man is comfortable calling his father 'John' and not 'Papa' like the African does. As a result of this there is moral decadence in the world today. Even at the jobsite, the man with a degree minimizes those without one.

Taku Victor: Your Highness! What do you suggest should be done to preserve our culture?

Fon Angwafor III: My son, in our days children moved closer to the elders to hear them talk and to learn more about their culture. By the fireside, they listened to the tales, parables and proverbs. Today a man is respected for having a doctorate degree but not for knowing his culture. A man is respected for his position and learning which are all foreign. In our days all learning was cultural. Today heroic achievements, bravery and humility are no longer respected.

Taku Victor: Your Highness, what do you propose by your wisdom as a way of reviving the storytelling event?

Fon Angwafor III:

This practice can no longer take place in the evenings. Some of our elders should be invited to tell the stories in schools with the aid of the Parent Teacher Associations. It will be impossible to rally people in their compounds and even in our palaces to tell stories. During our days, schools were rare and only those who went to school could speak English fluently. Today schools are everywhere and so homework and studies occupy the evenings. Even when my children are not studying, they are sitting watching movies on television and video decks. I suggest that academic authorities make provision for some aspects of the culture to be taught to the youths in schools. I propose the creation of vernacular radio stations to record and transmit stories and other values of the culture. The nation is the child. What a child grows up with is more permanent than what the adult tries to learn. So, the school curriculum is also an important instrument of preserving our culture and customs. We should learn to be patriotic, and to respect our culture and tradition. If we don't respect our tradition, we mock our ancestors and our place of birth.

Taku Victor: Your Highness, thank you for taking off your valuable time to shower me with words of wisdom.

Fon Angwafor III: My son, I will do all to see that our culture is preserved and respected. May God bless you in your research endeavours.

Interview with George D. Nyamndi, author of

Things Fall in Place carried out by Taku Victor on 25th February, 2015.

Taku Victor: You are a playwright, teacher, politician and critic. What are some of the plays that you've written and that are inspired by the socio-cultural, economic and political realities of Cameroon?

G.D. Nyamndi: I think basically all my plays derive their inspiration from happenings in society both immediate and distant, in terms of time and place. Playwriting as you know is quiet simply a particular look taken at society with a view to dramatizing some of the main features, some of its happenings that mark and give direction to our individual and collective life.

Taku Victor: Is *Things Fall in Place* based on an adaptation of a true or fictional African experience?

G.D. Nyamndi: *Things Fall in Place* reminds us of Chinua Achebe's very important work *Things Fall Apart*. My drama piece is an adaptation of that narrative for stage production. I think it is based on both aspects of experience: fictional and real. It is based on fictional experience in the sense that it adapts a fictional narrative *Things Fall Apart* for stage performance. But it is real in the sense that *Things Fall Apart* is, in itself, a realist novel. It centres around a time, place, people and a culture whose history we can identify. So, in essence, "Things Fall in Place" is both realist and fictional.

Taku Victor: Why things fall in place?

G.D. Nyamndi: We know that *Things Fall Apart* chronicles the falling apart of a way of life, of a culture and of a system. Time has passed and society has enriched itself with ways, ideas and ideologies from elsewhere. So, there is a sense in which we can say that the fictional universe of Achebe's 1954 novel has acquired a new dimension that qualifies it for modernity. You know that some of the ills that the novel highlights no longer occur in the traditional society that the novel looks at. And so we think that to that extent things that Achebe wrote have now fallen in place if that society is now in the hands of traditional people themselves. So "Things Fall in Place" is a symmetrical answer to the originating *Things Fall Apart*.

Taku Victor: Is *Things Fall in Place* a reflection of what is happening in other cultures of Africa?

G.D. Nyamndi: I should think so. *Things Fall Apart* did not chronicle the mishaps only of Achebe's cultural space. His fiction carries a symbolic meaning in the sense that what happens in it happens elsewhere too in other African societies. I think that Umuofia is a scaled-down version of Africa at the time Chinua Achebe wrote. So if things fell apart in Umuofia, they did fall apart equally in other Umuofias in other parts of Africa. So hopefully the ills that occasioned *Things Fall Apart* both at the micro and at the macro levels have been removed and things have also fallen in place in all those other places. That's my wish.

Taku Victor: Can we say that the chiefs and fons in Cameroon are in control because things have fallen in place?

G.D. Nyamndi: That's a tricky question because there is no such thing as a uniform chiefdom practice. Every context has its own defining norms for its chiefdom. In Cameroon, unlike in Nigeria, chiefs are brought under the umbrella of the administration and that is a practice which limits their authority and their grip on cultural reality rather seriously. In most places, chiefs are supplanted by administrative officials such as Governors, DOs or their assistants, which means that the people are torn in allegiance between traditional and administrative authority. That creates quite a problem. So, things fall in place, but they do so with new challenges. We are not saying that the apocalypse as it were of *Things Fall Apart* has now been replaced by a utopian feel of things. What we are saying is that society has evolved and that the evolution carries elements of development but also germs of destruction which must be handled with care. What we are also saying is that the chiefdoms that continue to exercise some kind of control over their respective polities are dwindling with each passing day as inroads continue to be made into their traditional space by administrative authority. That relationship has to be reviewed occasionally to ensure that nobody oversteps their boundaries.

Taku Victor: What inspired you to choose Chinua Achebe's novel as the basis for your adaptation?

G.D. Nyamndi: Firstly the novel spoke to me in a very immediate way as it ought to speak to every African. And I thought that the best way of indicating my own

appreciation to Achebe was in diversifying the pedagogic potentials of the novel. Because it is not only literature but also a therapeutic instrument for Africans; a narrative that speaks to our sense of pride. Now, if we leave it to the novel's sphere only, it will not reach out to as many readers as its importance warrants. And so I thought that if we could place it on stage, we would by so doing be diversifying its potential to reach out to a large public and to make its message a lot more immediate than it is in narrative form because you know that theatre is a lot more direct and more powerful in its message delivery potential than the novel because in the former you come face-to-face with re-enacted reality or re-enacted problems and challenges. That way you can gauge the importance of that narrative immediately without flipping pages upon pages.

Taku Victor: Can we say that *Things Fall Apart* has reached its target audience?

G.D. Nyamndi: That's a rhetorical question. As I said, it cannot reach enough readers. We cannot place our finger on the number that *Things Fall Apart* was intended to reach. What we can say for sure is that the more readers the novel reaches the better for African culture. That's why we should stop at nothing to sustain the outreach drive of that message because *Things Fall Apart* is addressed first of all to Africans. Whether or not it has reached the readers or playgoers it set out to reach is of quite some immediate importance to me. What I know is even more important is that we continue to encourage and facilitate the narrative's outreach potential.

Taku Victor: What are the benefits of adapting from one literary genre to another?

G.D. Nyamndi: I think the advantages are many, even if they come with creative challenges. The very first one is that to adapt you must first of all be won over by the source genre as it were; in this case the novel. If the novel does not speak to you, you won't go beyond readership into that second stage that consists in transforming yourself into a vehicle of whatever message the novel intends to send out. Now, in adapting, the tendency is to move from a broader narrative texture to a more concise, more immediate, streamlined version; in this case drama. So, when you adapt, you also remove some of the less urgent, some of the less important aspects of the novel narrative form and you go for a message that is dramatized. Drama is all about dramatizing message, dramatizing issues of immediate importance. So I think that when you adapt, the basic motivation is to make the message more immediate and more available to a wider public. And that way you dramatize not only what the novel says, but the potential effect of what it says on the audience or the reader as the case may be. So, there are, as I say, immediate gains, immediate advantages, immediate reasons for wanting to adapt. But the pre-condition for that adaptation is interest in the original document. If I had read *Things Fall Apart* and not found it worth my while, I wouldn't have bothered going into that second stage of adapting it.

Taku Victor: Do you need permission from the novelist, original/source writer or the production house in order to adapt?

G.D. Nyamndi: Frankly, I didn't address my mind to that. Once a work has been produced, it now falls in the public domain and people can do what they like with it. Novels have occasioned films, debates, musicals, theatre pieces etc. I do not think that each time you approach a writing from one of these diversified angles, you need to go back to whoever to find out if you need to use the work or not. Once you write, you surrender the product to the reading public and it is for them to decide what to do with the work.

Taku Victor: What were some of your challenges of adapting *Things Fall Apart* into *Thing Fall in Place*?

G.D. Nyamndi: I had quite a few of them probably because my own cultural background is not very similar to Achebe's. I needed a good dose of empathy to bring alive the cultural referents in *Things Fall Apart* and shape them in such a way as to suit them for stage production. Secondly, emphasis becomes a problem. The person adapting, and who is not necessarily from the environment in which the novel is set, may miss some fine points, may misinterpret or misjudge some elements and maybe misplace emphasis. You may stress or emphasize an aspect that shouldn't be stressed or you may overlook other important elements. Whether we like it or not, our own culture or upbringing interferes in the adaptation process, so that the end product cannot be equal to the source text. That's why adaptations are different, and they produce different effects. No two people would produce the same adaptation because external factors come into play and do affect the end product, to which we must add our own challenges, preferences, temperaments, ideologies which also colour the universe of our drama.

Taku Victor: Do you encourage young adapting artists to visit the society in which the story is set before attempting to embark on adaptation?

G.D. Nyamndi: Yes and no. Yes, in the sense that Nigeria is well advanced in that area. And if we want good expertise on adaptation, Nigeria is the place to go to because I think that local playwrights, local text manipulators can very well do their work without necessarily relying on outside influence. The person adapting the text is always the best interpreter of that text, at that given moment. If you want to rely too much on external influence, there is the danger that over- reliance may result in influence and that influence will also affect the originality of your production. We want to see the different and differentiated temperaments in the adaptation. I come from a cultural sphere that is very masculine in its attitude. And so my adaptation may betray some sympathy with someone like Okonkwo in the novel whereas somebody from a more sedate environment, from a more likeable culture will also want to tone down or be less receptive to the actions of the protagonist. So where our young artists can, for example, get enrichment from, let them do so. But that should not be a pre-condition for them to forge ahead with what is beneficial to our society.

Taku Victor: What is your target audience?

G.D. Nyamndi: My target audience is everybody because that play has a pedagogic mission. It is there to show us the importance of ourselves being the authors of our own destinies and being the first estates as it were, the admirers of our own specific cultural values. And so that kind of message does not select its audience. It can let Africans be the priority audience; but we do not lose anything by expanding that audience to include other cultural sensibilities.

Taku Victor: Are there any new elements that you brought in that are different from what Achebe uses in his novel?

G.D. Nyamndi: Yes, certainly. For things to fall in place, you have to make them fall in place. And so in *Things Fall in Place*, at the end of the play, a memorial is founded in honour of Okonkwo, The Okonkwo Memorial, which is a school where the likes of his son, Nwoye, who could not go to school because of his father's trenchant opposition to Western values, can now attend school. Do not forget that everybody in *Things Fall Apart* is a symbol and that little boy carries with him some of the tragedies that we see in African societies today, such as the denial of access to education for reasons which are usually untenable. Ikemefuna and other little children are sacrificed on the altar of practices in today's world that have little or no locus standi. In *Things Fall in Place*, we pool all the parts together in this Memorial. So we can say that Okonkwo lived for an ideal, that ideal not being necessarily what he thought it to be but rather what the society that lived after him said it was. The Okonkwo Memorial is built with the money used to obtain temporary release of the village elders. That's the money which goes into that project. So in essence, what we are saying here is that Africans are really the authors of their own destinies.

Taku Victor: How enriching are our oral sources in the process of adaptation?

G.D. Nyamndi: You cannot remove the influence of the oral source from the written narrative in Africa. If oral sources inform and direct written texts, we can also conclude that they are important in adaptive exercises. Now the first thing that we say about orality is that it takes us back into the traditional environment itself. You can tell when, for example, Achebe uses proverbs. Those proverbs do not come from texts. They are orality in expression. In proverbs you actually see traditional life in progress. And you see the elders, you see the different castes, structures, so that quite simply looking at the proverbs you can portray, you can paint the structural picture of the society you are dealing with. Songs, dances and rituals are elements of orality without which local colour that is one of the basic attractions of these African texts and productions wouldn't be there. If we want to go for local colour, it is to orality that we first of all have to look because it is orality that constitutes the gauge, the receptacle of traditional values; so that if we know that we are dealing with an oral culture, we will also be better able to understand the thinking, the ideology, and the practices of that culture. And we will be better able to accommodate what to somebody from a written tradition may look like a digression. Orality depends on memorative transmission. So quite often you hear one story here today and tomorrow you hear a different version of that same story. The memory on which those versions depend also has its own weaknesses and idiosyncrasies that affect the oral production.

Taku Victor: What do you advise budding script-writers as far as going back to their oral traditions in an attempt to enrich their script is concerned?

G.D. Nyamndi: I do not know whether we can be prescriptive in this respect. Much of what the script-writer does would depend on what he wants to produce. It is not all; let's not forget that orality does not exercise exclusive control over life in Africa. There are cases in which orality may even be considered an endangered practice. Now, if a script-writer is interested in traditional life, sure he will need to rely on the deep oral repertoire of that particular culture. But if you have a script-writer who is interested in urbanity, you will not expect him to go looking for orality in an urban environment even though urban orality too exists. But I think it does so in a less important manner than it does in the traditional settings where cultural transmission is still basically by word of mouth. So I would encourage them to use orality, where orality reveals itself as a useful tool of creative achievement. But the use of orality should not be forced. If your character is an educated person, you will be wary in the way you subject him to the resources of orality. And so what you do with orality is consequent on the type of text that you want to produce.

Taku Victor: In this present context of play production and theatre-going, are you hopeful that your play will get to its destined audience?

G.D. Nyamndi: I remain very hopeful. The only problem is that theatre is very economy sensitive. Theatre going in the West is a very rich practice because the west is an affluent society. Theatre is a leisure activity. It is not

an obligatory function. So you go to the theatre when everything else has been taken care of. And I think that's where our biggest problem is. Africans are not theatre-goers because they are too embroiled in the daily business of survival. Even if the gate fee is a 100 FRS, it may sound small but there are families that cannot raise that kind of money to feed themselves. So you do not expect them to abandon the urgent matters of feeding the family and use whatever little money they have to go to the theatre. Now, there is reason to be hopeful, since economic progress is on the list of all governments. So let's hope that as things improve theatre-going too will improve and the message will reach out to a wider public.

Taku Victor: Can the radio play and educational theatre be employed for now?

G.D. Nyamndi: What I say about theatre goes for radio. How many Cameroonians listen to the radio? When they come back from wherever they went to look for the means to survive, they are generally so worn out, so exhausted that the only thing they want is food and then they reach for their little beds and that's the end of the day. As I say, theatre, radio for community outreach, all these will come to the centre of message dissemination as the economic situation of the society improves. These things are very dependent on the economy. I mean the economy here in a much broader context which includes democracy, health and governance; the economy as the synthesis of all the conditions that make for good human existence.

Taku Victor: Thank you very much, Sir, for taking off time to throw more light on the concept of adaptation and your experiences adapting Chinua Achebe's *Things Fall Apart* to *Things Fall in Place*.

List of Informants

Names	Social status	Sex	Village
Emmanuel Dikabo Bebe II	Chief	M	Banga-Bakundu
Mesumbe Anthony	Chief	M	Muantah-Muambong
S.N. Ejedepang-Koge	Notable/ teacher	M	Tombel
Noupea Nkayimbo Margaret Assumpta	Teacher	F	Bandjoun
Taku Peter Nembo	Nkweta	M	Agong-Mangang
Samuel Moka Lifafa Endeley	Chief	M	Bokwaongo, Buea
Dr. Eben Njang Simon	Church elder	M	Great Soppo, Buea
Winston Sama Fonyonga	Prince	M	Bali-Nyongha
Lekunze Jacob	Notable	M	Bamumbu
Ngeh Andrew Tata	Sub-chief	M	Ndu

Names	Social status	Sex	Village
LImen Fenkwai Peter	Sub-chief	M	Njamchep, Bawok- Bali
Nsuh Francis Tumensang	Notable	M	Funtah, Mbeba-li- Bafut
Daniel Asongwe	Prince	M	Ntingkag-Man-kon
Fon Angwafor III	Fon	M	Mankon
Ngobu Daniel Gweh	Teacher	M	Mbe-soh-Bamessing
James Bebanghia	Notable	M	Mbe-soh-Bamessing

Names	Social status	Sex	Village
Che Michael	Driver	M	Ntingkag-Mankon
Fru Isidore	Shoemak-er	M	Ntingkag-Mankon
Gweh Amadine	Student	F	Mbesoh-Bamess-ing
Kubang Shelly	Student	F	Mbesoh-Bamess-ing

Names	Social status	Sex	Village
Frida Lumah	House-wife	F	Wokoko-Buea
Effange Ophelia	Clerk	F	Soppo-Buea
Ebeneze Nwendi Litumbe	Notable	M	Wokoko-Buea
Joseph Njombo Abwa-Mboh	Teacher	M	Kumba Town

Index